The Layman's Bible Study Series

Hagar of Egypt

A Perspective on Strength, Courage & Faith

Jim Melanson

I0163909

Hagar of Egypt: A Perspective on Strength, Courage, and Faith

The Layman's Bible Study Series

© 2017 by James Melanson

Printed by CreateSpace

Available for Kindle, Kobo and other eReaders

ISBN: 978-0-9937565-4-2

More titles available at:

www.jimmelanson.ca

Editorial service provided by Dorathy Gass

www.metwritingservices.com

Cover image licensed from iStockPhoto.Com.

Stock illustration ID:503783259

Dedication

For my Mom.

I miss you.

Chapter 1

Introduction

In this book, I am going to explore the story of Hagar, the princess (arguably, a slave) that was gifted to the House of Abram by Pharaoh. These events are recounted in the book of Genesis in the Holy Bible. When I started studying Genesis, I became both entranced and fascinated by the story of this woman, her child, and the events impacting the formation of her faith; her spiritual formation to use a more modern term.

There is much about Hagar that reminds me of my own mother, whom I lost in 2011. Both Hagar and my mother shared similar traits that let her persevere through some very difficult times. I think this is why I have been so drawn to the story of Hagar, one of the strongest women I have encountered in the Holy Bible. Her lessons of strength, courage, and faith are all words that described my own mother's journey through life.

My study and research have taken a biblical story from an ancient time and put it in the perspective of modern life in a way that I can relate to personally. In having a firsthand view of what a single mother can go through mentally, emotionally, and financially; I have connected with this story in a way that makes it come alive. I watched my mother in a difficult marriage. I saw her working jobs that she came home from and her fingers were literally bleeding from the work she did. I watched her scramble, fight, persevere, and never give up. The two things that kept her going were her love for me, and her faith in God.

I believe that Abram/Abraham is a role model of faith and perseverance for all of the Abrahamic religions and that he is the Pentateuch's (first five books of the Old Testament) inspirational "every-man." I also believe that Hagar is an inspiration for all of us, especially those who are cornered into circumstances requiring them to face the world head-on and emotionally alone. Hagar is a role model for those who have control taken away from them, irrespective of gender. The lessons we learn from her apply equally to readers of any faith.

The story of Hagar has many modern equivalents: spouses and children being abandoned, sexual exploitation, adolescent vulnerability, teen pregnancy, difficult family dynamics, bullying, etc.

For Christian and Jewish readers, the story of Hagar is pivotal to the story of Sarai's faith, or lack thereof, and the eventual demonstration of God's power through opening her womb. For Muslim readers, Hagar is the mother of the Prophet Ishmael, and her story is the nexus of these three faiths. While Christian and Jewish readers will be familiar with Abraham from the Old Testament, they may not know he is spoken of as a "role model" in the Noble Quran (Surah An-Nahl 16:120-123):

120. Abraham was indeed a model, Devoutly obedient to God, (And) true in faith, and he Joined not gods with God

121. He showed his gratitude For the favours of God, Who chose him, and guided him To a Straight Way.

122. And We gave him Good In this world, and he will be, In the Hereafter, in the ranks Of the Righteous,

123. So We have taught thee The inspired (message), "Follow the ways of Abraham The True in Faith, and he Joined not gods with God."

In Judaism, Abraham is the first patriarch of the Judaism. He is the one that received the covenant that all practising Jews are bound to. Author Rabbi Dr Nissan Mindel writes[1]:

"At the age of three, as our sages tell us (Nedarim 32a), Abraham recognized that there was, is, and will be but one G-d, the creator of heaven and earth. Abraham dedicated his whole life to spreading the knowledge of G-d. G-d was one and only in the heavens (on earth no as yet knew Him, except Abraham), and Abraham was the one and only man on earth who knew G-d and worshipped Him. Abraham was known as "Ho-Ivri" - "the Hebrew," which also means "the-one-on-the-other-side" - because all the world was on one side, and he alone was on the other. But soon the "G-d of Abraham" came to be known by more and more people. Every man who left Abraham's tent, and every woman who left Sarah's tent, had learned something about G-d, and went away blessing the "G-d of Abraham." Even to this day, when we address ourselves to G-d in our Shemone-esrei

3

prayer three times daily, we pray to the "G-d of Abraham, the G-d of Isaac and the G-d of Jacob, …"

For the reasons, Abraham is important to Jews, so too is he important to Christians. As well, according to the genealogies in the gospels of Matthew and Luke, Jesus Christ is a descendant of Abraham. The story of Abraham and Isaac and the almost-sacrifice is an important story of faith for all three religions, though in Islam the story has Ishmael being sacrificed instead of Isaac.

In Islam, Abraham is called the "messenger of God" and is considered a prophet. The Prophet Muhammad is a direct descendant of Abraham through Ishmael, the child he conceived with Hagar. "Islam considers Abraham to be "one of the first Muslims" (the Noble Quran - Surah Ali 'Imran 3:66-68), the first monotheist in a world where monotheism was lost, and the community of those faithful to God …"[2]

With the story of Hagar, we find that the Abrahamic religions share a common story with common themes and meanings:

- Faith.
- God is infinite in His wisdom, and we are not.
- God loves us and never abandons us.
- All things transpire according to God's will and timing.
- God declares Himself.

If you have not read the story of Hagar in the Holy Bible, I have included the relevant chapters from the

4

book of Genesis at the back of this book in the section titled "Excerpts from the Book of Genesis".

I truly hope you derive as much joy and affirmation from this exploration of the story of Hagar of Egypt, as I did through studying, researching, and writing this humble perspective.

Sources & Conventions

Bible Version

In this text, the bible quotes (unless otherwise specified) are taken from the New International Version (NIV). If you have the King James Version (KJV), the wording will be slightly older style, but basically the same. For authority, I always refer to the KJV. However, for day-to-day study and worship I find the NIV keeps it simple, is usually understandable, and is accurately translated. When it comes to word study, that is, understanding the true meaning of a specific word, I always refer to the original Koine Greek that it was written in.

Focus on Islam

You may be wondering why a Christian author is talking about Islam in a book about a persona from the Holy Bible. The story of Hagar is also the story of the birth of Ishmael (Ismail). Hagar and Abraham's son, the half-brother of Isaac, is a prophet of Islam. The story of Hajar (Hagar) and Ishmael have slight variations in the Islamic sources. As an example, in the Noble Quran (37:100-109), it was Ismail and not Isaac that was bound and almost sacrificed on the altar. As both were the son of Abraham, it doesn't change the meaning of the story, just the perspective. Many Arabs consider themselves descendant from Ishmael; even the Islamic Prophet Mohammed (author of the Noble Quran) claims descent from Ishmael. There is also a great deal of historical tradition about the Prophet Ismail (Ishmael) within the ancient texts of Islam just as there is in the ancient texts of Judaism. While none of the Islamic or Jewish traditions about Ishmael alters our story, they do offer some interesting colour during our examination of the story, and its meaning to us today.

The Noble Quran

In this text, quotes from the Noble Quran are taken from www.sacred-texts.com/isl/quran/

Genesis Rabbah

The Genesis Rabbah (properly called the Bereshit Rabbah) is a religious text from the classical period of Judaism. It is a midrash (body of homiletic stories) of focused homiletic exegesis concerning the book of Genesis. It was written in the first half of the 4th century by the amora (someone who conveyed information verbally rather than by written word) Hoshaiah (not to be confused with Hosea).

Sahih Bukhari

The Sahih Bukhari is a collection of hadith (also known as the Sunnah), a collection of sayings and actions by the Islamic Prophet Mohammed. Written in the first half of the 9th century, to extremely high standards, it is stated by Ibn el-Neil, "Bukhari's collection is recognised by the overwhelming majority of the Muslim world to be one of the most authentic collections of the Sunnah of the Prophet."

Date Systems

As I relate this story to you, I will be giving specific dates. Because a lot of dates this far back can be a matter of opinion, varying by many years, I felt compelled to use a baseline reference. For this reason, all of the dates in this book are based on the content of *Annals of the World*. It was originally written in 1658 by Bishop Ussher of Ireland and re-published this century by Master Books (2003), edited by Larry and Marion Pierce. I will provide the recognisable BCE (Before Common Era) date and then in brackets will provide the Anno Mundi date for perspective (literally meaning "in the year of the world", it references the number of years following creation, as in Genesis 1:1). This means that the date of Abram's birth would be 1996 BCE (2008 AM). 2008 AM would be 2,008 years after Creation according to the date system used by Bishop Ussher.

Abram versus Abraham

You will note in this text I refer to Abraham as both Abram and Abraham. I have tried to keep the proper name in the context of where it appears in the story of this text. Abraham was indeed born with the name Abram (Gen 11:26). In Gen 17:5 God changes Abram's name to Abraham, meaning "father of a multitude" because God is going to make him a father of many nations.

You will also have Sarah's name initially as Sarai. In Gen 17:15, God tells Abraham that his wife Sarai (meaning "princess") will now be called Sarah (meaning "queen") because He will make her the mother of many nations and that kings of people will be "of" her, meaning they will be her descendants.

In reference to Islamic text, I may refer to Abraham as Ibrahim who is revered as an Islamic prophet.

There is some difference of opinion in Christian and Islamic circles whether a Christian should use the phrase "Peace be upon him" or "Upon him be peace" after mentioning the name of a prophet of Islam. I am a Christian, but I write to a Christian, Jewish, and Muslim audience. Please understand that I do not intend to offend anyone with my decision not to include that phrase specifically within the text of this book. I do not do so out of disrespect, rather because in the understanding of my faith it is not required. I do, however, wish that "peace be upon *everyone*".

Chapter 2
Hagar's Story

Author's note: Looking solely at the text of the Holy Bible, the rich, deep and meaningful story of Hagar takes up little space though it covers many years. This is my narrative based on the story as found in the book of Genesis. You can also find the story, slightly expanded on, in The Works of Josephus (1.12.1-4)[3]. Here is a short narrative of the story of Hagar.

Abram, his family, and his household along with his nephew Lot's family and household travel to Egypt. They do this to escape the famine that was, at that time, rampant in their homeland. Because Abram is afraid that he will be killed when the Egyptians see how beautiful Sarai his wife is, he pulls a ruse. Abram has Sarai claim to be his sister rather than his wife. While Abram does survive and not get killed, the Pharaoh also happens to take a shine to Abram's "sister". Sarai, Abram's wife, is, in fact, his half-sister (same father, different mother), but that's not important to the story as wife trumps sister in the relationship. Pharaoh takes Sarai into his house and shortly, suffering God's wrath for his sin, learns the truth. He learns that Sarai is Abram's wife. A bit mad about this, yet still contrite due to God's vengeance, he gives Sarai the present of a personal servant, a handmaid named Hagar. Hagar also happens to be the Pharaoh's daughter (I will deal with this idea later in the book). Having already showered Abram with gifts of cattle and such, Pharaoh then sends the whole lot of them out of Egypt.

Fast forward a few years, Abram and Sarai have been promised a child by God, but as yet, none has been conceived. Abram and Sarai are quite old at this point, so old that Sarai has passed her childbearing ability. Not believing it is now possible for God to give them a child between them (Abram and Sarai), Sarai offers her regal handmaid Hagar to her husband to conceive a child with. He agrees, and in a short time, Hagar has conceived.

Regardless that it was her idea, Sarai quickly grows to despise Hagar for her ability to give her (Sarai's) husband a child. As well, Sarai becomes despised in the eyes of her handmaid. Things get worse and worse between Hagar and Sarai to the point that Hagar finally has to flee the household. She sets off into the desert on her own. Travelling to a certain point, she stops and rests by a spring of water. It is here that she encounters an angel of the Lord who asks her where she is going and why. The angel then tells her to go back to where she came from, do what she has to do, and put up with what she has to put up with. The angel then tells her she is going to have a son and the son will be named Ishmael. Hagar acknowledges God and then returns to the household she had just fled from. As promised, she has the child when Abram is eighty-six years old, and Abram names the child Ishmael, as was foretold by the angel.

In a matter of time, God fulfils his promise to Abraham and Sarah. He opens Sarah's womb, and she conceives a child with her husband. When the child is born, he is named Isaac. After a few years, there comes the point where Sarah can no longer stand having Ishmael around. She does not want Ishmael, the son of the handmaiden and her husband, to take the double share of inheritance due to the firstborn or any inheritance amount for that matter, from her husband, Abraham. She convinces Abraham to send Hagar and the child away from the household, away from the family, to banish them to the desert. Abraham, heavy of heart about this, seeks wisdom and guidance from God who tells him to go ahead and do as Sarah asks. Abraham does this, sending Hagar and her son, his son, off into the Negev Desert with a loaf of bread and a bottle of water.

With the water soon gone and reaching a crisis point where she is convinced her young son is going to die, Hagar places him in the shade of a bush and then walks far away from him so that she doesn't hear the sounds of death coming upon him. Again, an angel of God appears to Hagar. He tells her to pluck up, things are going to be okay and oh by the way, here is a well of water for you. She takes the water, revitalised her son with it, and off they go. God is with the boy as he grows up, his mother finds him a wife and all works out in the end for Hagar.

Chapter 3

Hagar: Historical Character or Literary Figure?

Was Hagar Real?

Alluded to in the New Testament (Galatians 4:21-31), the story of Hagar can be found in the first book of The Holy Bible, in the book of Genesis (16:1-16, 21:9-21). Hagar is also found in the Torah (Gen. 16:1-16, 21:9-21) and is alluded to in The Noble Quran (Surah Ibrahim 14:37).

There is a midrash which identifies Hagar as Keturah, who married Abraham after Sarah's death[4,5].

There are several entries in the Sahih Bukhari that refer to Hagar. Supporting the story of her presentation to Abram's wife Sarai by Pharaoh, we read this in (Vol.4, Book 55) Hadith 578:

> "The tyrant then gave Hajar as a girl-servant to Sarah. Sarah came back (to Abraham) while he was praying. Abraham, gesturing with his hand, asked, "What has happened?" She replied, "Allah has spoiled the evil plot of the infidel (or immoral person) and gave me Hajar for service."

The story of Hagar and Ishmael's expulsion is confirmed in another hadith, in which I found a slight twist to the story that is told in The Holy Bible. In Genesis 21:14 Abraham sends Hagar and Ishmael away; it says, *"she departed, and wandered in the*

13

wilderness of Beer-Sheba". Illustrators have typically depicted this as Hagar and Ishmael leaving the camp of Abraham on their own. It is generally accepted in any readings I have done on this passage, that Abraham did not accompany them. However, depending on how loosely you interpret the passage, it does not specifically say that he did not accompany them any of the distance they travelled. I raise this point simply because of an intriguing entry in the Sahih Bukhari, (Vol.4, Book 55) Hadith 584:

> "When Abraham had differences with his wife, (because of her jealousy of Hajar, Ishmael's mother), he took Ishmael and his mother and went away. They had a water-skin with them containing some water, Ishmael's mother used to drink water from the water-skin so that her milk would increase for her child. When Abraham reached Mecca, he made her sit under a tree and afterwards returned home. Ishmael's mother followed him, and when they reached Kada, she called him from behind, "O Abraham! To whom are you leaving us?" He replied, "(I am leaving you) to Allah's (Care)." She said, "I am satisfied to be with Allah."

Now we ask ourselves the question, was Hagar a real person? We have religious text from three different faiths referring to the same person. The Holy Bible, the Genesis Rabbah, and the Sahih Bukhari all say she was a real person. While we are studying her story from the Holy Bible, we have to recognise that she is also alluded to in the primary text of Islam, the Noble Quran. The only thing we are missing is physical evidence.

14

Sadly, we do not have any archaeological findings relating to Hagar or Keturah. However, we do have references to Abraham (Abram). The name, Abraham, has been found in Babylonian texts of the sixteenth century in the form "Abamram", and in other forms at Mari. A Mari text also uses the name of Abraham's brother, Nahor, in the form "Nakhur" as the name of a city in the vicinity of Haran. We find references in Josephus 1.7.2 that Abram is also mentioned by Berosus, Hecataeus, and Nicolaus of Damascus.

While there is no direct archaeological evidence as yet to confirm or deny the existence of Abraham or Hagar, the last century has seen many advances in the science of archaeology and many new findings. There is always the possibility that we will eventually have archaeological evidence for these Biblical characters. Aside from direct physical evidence, the basic presupposition of all Christians is that the Holy Bible is the inspired word of God and therefore, infallible. The Holy Bible tells us that Hagar was, in fact, a real person and the story related about her is true. The Islamic community, who don't believe in the Holy Bible, believe that Hagar was indeed real as they revere her as the wife of the Prophet Ibrahim (Abraham) and the mother of the Prophet Ismail (Ishmael). The Jewish community as well, considers that Hagar was real, just as Abraham was.

The only sensible question being raised of Hagar being from Egypt comes from *The Works of Philo*. Philo was a Hellenistic-Jewish philosopher who lived in Alexandria, Egypt during the time of Christ. In his works, he poses the thought that perhaps Sarai was saying (Gen 16:1) that Hagar was Egyptian in her nature and philosophy rather than physically from Egypt[6]. However, the Holy Bible, the quoted midrash, and the quoted hadith would be at odds with this.

What about Keturah

A person by the name of Keturah (as Abraham's second wife) appears in Genesis chapter 25. The Genesis Rabbah asserts that Keturah is Hagar, though there is some contention on this belief.

We also find the name Keturah as Abraham's concubine in 1 Chronicles 1:32-33.

It is quite possible that Abraham maintained contact with Hagar and Ishmael. This possibility arises in the story of Abraham's binding of Isaac (the Akeda) for sacrifice, where we find an interesting question emerge beginning with how this story is interpreted in Judaism. The text of Genesis 22:3 (KJV) says:

> *"And Abraham rose up early in the morning, and saddled his ass, and took two of his young men with him, and Isaac his son, and clave the wood for the burnt offering, and rose up, and went unto the place of which God had told him."*

In the NIV version, the text reads

> *"Early the next morning Abraham got up and loaded his donkey. He took with him two of his servants and his son Isaac. When he had cut enough wood for the burnt offering, he set out for the place God had told him about."*

While I think it's fairly clear in the KJV and NIV that two servants accompanied Abram and Isaac to the place the sacrifice was to occur, we find a different interpretation in Judaism. Rabbi Moshe Reiss, Oxford graduate and former assistant Rabbi at Yale University, puts forth the following in his article, *"Ishmael, Son of Abraham"* (reprinted with permission):

> "When Abraham takes Isaac to the akeda whom does he bring with him - two young men; in Jewish tradition they are the servant Eliezer and the brother Ishmael.[i] It would seem that Abraham told Eliezer to go to Ishmael's home and ask him to meet them on the road. It is unclear how old Isaac and Ishmael were at the time of the akeda. According to Jewish lore Isaac was an adult. It is unlikely that Abraham would request Ishmael to meet him if they had no relationship for many years. Abraham probably kept that relationship a secret from Sarah. He also did not tell Sarah of the pending akeda. His father did not suddenly remember Ishmael, but must have had a secret relationship with him.
>
> Why did Abraham ask Ishmael to go with him? Did he feel that if Isaac were going to die he wanted his other son, his only remaining son with him? Did he consider that Ishmael could become the son of the promise? After the akeda Abraham sends Ishmael back home since he cannot have him appear at Sarah's.
>
> What did Isaac think of Ishmael coming at his father's request to his slaughtering? What did Isaac think of his brother Ishmael, who his mother

considered illegitimate, unwanted and dangerous? Did he think his father thought that Ishmael would replace him?

After burying Sarah, Abraham, according to Jewish midrashim goes to visit Ishmael, but he is out hunting. His Egyptian wife seeing an old man she did not know sends him away. Abraham seems utterly alone. Sarah is dead, Isaac is traumatized from the akeda, Ishmael is not home and Ishmael's wife sends him away. But when Ishmael comes home his wife tells him of the old man, he realizes it is Abraham his father and sends the Egyptian wife away. He remarries a Canaanite woman and sends a message to his father apologizing, telling him he has sent the wife away and begs him to come visit again.[ii]

Abraham realizes that he has to take care of his traumatized son Isaac. He understands that Isaac will not be capable of taking care of himself - he is damaged - as a result of Abraham and God. Abraham calls in his loyal servant Eliezer and tells him to go to back to his family and find a wife who can take care of Isaac.

After the marriage of Isaac and Rebekah Abraham, we are told then marries Keturah. Why does Abraham, an old man marry again? Does he find it difficult to live with his powerful daughter-in-law Rebekah and his weak son? In Jewish midrashim Keturah is Hagar![iii] He then goes to live with Ishmael. Ishmael, despite the great difficulty he and his mother had with his father's senior wife Sarah and his father's allowing this to take place, divorced a wife who was inhospitable to his father and took his old father in the last years of his life. Rashi (a medieval Jewish commentator) suggests that Isaac went to Hagar to have her marry his father, an attempt to compensate for what his mother had done to Hagar and his brother (Rashi on 24:62). In the Book of Jubilees (2nd century BCE) Ishmael and Isaac celebrate the festival of Pentecost together with their father.[iv]"

i   Ginsberg, L., Legends of the Jews, (JPS, Philadelphia, 1975) p. 129.
ii Ginsberg, pp. 123-125
iii Genesis Rabbah 61:4, pp.542-543
iv The Book of Jubilees, chapter 22.

While the Bible does not specifically address any further contact between Abraham and Hagar, that does not mean it did not happen. The above narrative by Rabbi Reis would be supported by the previously quoted Hadith 5849.

It is interesting to note that Josephus (1.15)[7] dictates that the children and grandchildren of Abraham and Hagar populated Troglodytes (which Clarke's Commentary claims is Egypt on the coast of the Red Sea[8]) and Arabia the Happy (Arabia Felix[9]).

If you have spent any time reading the Holy Bible, you will have observed that it will frequently sum up entire lives in only a few words or a few passages. To illustrate, after the mention of Abram's birth, we don't encounter Abram again until he is in his 70's. If we are to accept that Abraham and Hagar did maintain contact or that at least Abraham and Ishmael maintained contact, then perhaps this may put a bit more colour onto the story of Hagar and Ishmael's expulsion in Genesis 21. It would also support the theory that Keturah was, in fact, Hagar.

Was Hagar a historical character or a literary figure? In my heart, with the passion of my faith, I believe she was a historical character. Until the archaeological evidence comes forth, I can only assert that she is a literary character. Whether she was real or only an illustration, what is most relevant are the lessons we have been given the opportunity to learn through studying the Word of God and the lessons He presents for us in this story.

Chapter 4
Covenant, Famine & Deception

While the woman Hagar is the subject of this book, much of this story revolves around Abram and his wife, Sarai. To properly understand the arrival of Hagar within the house of Abram, we need to understand how Abram got to Egypt and the events that occurred upon his arrival.

Covenant

The covenant with Abraham called the Covenant of Circumcision in the NIV, occurs in Genesis 17. However, God starts leading up to this covenant starting in Genesis 12. In the intervening space, God promises land to Abram and his descendants and then adds more land to His original promise. God is also getting Abram used to the idea of many descendants. In the first few chapters of the accounts of Abram, already he was well into what we currently think of as old age. Abram and Sarai were childless; this fact is a pivotal point in the story of Hagar.

The first narration involving Abram occurs in Genesis 12. In this chapter, God tells Abram to leave his country, his family, and his father's house (Terah) and go to a land that He will lead him to (Gen 12:1). At the tender age of seventy-five, Abram, accompanied by his nephew Lot, took his wife, his house, and his possessions and headed south from

Harran. Lot's wife, house, servants, and possessions travelled with them as well. They first went to Canaan, then to the hills east of Bethel, and then on to the Negev (Gen 12:5-9). Having already promised Abram that He would make of him a great nation (Gen 12:2), while on a stopover in Canaan, God promises that this land will be given to his seed, his descendants (Gen 12: 6-7):

> *"Abram traveled through the land as far as the site of the great tree of Moreh at Shechem. At that time the Canaanites were in the land. The Lord appeared to Abram and said, "To your offspring I will give this land." So he built an altar there to the Lord, who had appeared to him."*

The Lord expands on the original covenant by better defining the area He is going to give Abram's descendants in Genesis 13: 14-17:

> *The Lord said to Abram after Lot had parted from him, "Look around from where you are, to the north and south, to the east and west. All the land that you see I will give to you and your offspring forever. I will make your offspring like the dust of the earth, so that if anyone could count the dust, then your offspring could be counted. Go, walk through the length and breadth of the land, for I am giving it to you."*

The promise has more land added to it in Genesis 15: 18-21:

> *On that day the Lord made a covenant with Abram and said, "To your descendants I give this land, from the Wadi of Egypt to the great river, the Euphrates— the land of the Kenites, Kenizzites,*

Kadmonites, Hittites, Perizzites, Rephaites, Amorites, Canaanites, Girgashites and Jebusites."

This promise, this covenant is repeated to Moses in Exodus 6:5-8:

Moreover, I have heard the groaning of the Israelites, whom the Egyptians are enslaving, and I have remembered my covenant. "Therefore, say to the Israelites: 'I am the Lord, and I will bring you out from under the yoke of the Egyptians. I will free you from being slaves to them, and I will redeem you with an outstretched arm and with mighty acts of judgment. I will take you as my own people, and I will be your God. Then you will know that I am the Lord your God, who brought you out from under the yoke of the Egyptians. And I will bring you to the land I swore with uplifted hand to give to Abraham, to Isaac and to Jacob. I will give it to you as a possession. I am the Lord.'
"

The covenant is finally fulfilled roughly 500 years after the original promise to Abraham. It is fulfilled in Joshua chapter 1. However, it is filled after the four hundred years that Israel and the Children of Israel (all Abraham's descendants through Isaac) were held as slave labour in Egypt which was prophesied in Genesis 15:13-14:

Then the Lord said to him, "Know for certain that for four hundred years your descendants will be strangers in a country not their own and that they will be enslaved and mistreated there. But I will punish the nation they serve as slaves, and afterward they will come out with great possessions."

As part of the Abrahamic Covenant, God promises to make a great nation from him (Abram). In Biblical parlance, making a great nation of a person refers to their descendants and their descendants of those. It doesn't necessarily mean a holy nation or a powerful nation; it means a nation of many people, a nation with many, many pairs of hands and feet. In the ancient Near East (roughly the Middle Bronze Age), bigger would definitely be better.

The importance of this to the story of Hagar is that a very great expectation was placed within the spirit of both Abram and his wife Sarai, the expectation of children. However, as our story unfolds, Abram and Sarai have no children. Sarai has grown to an age (late 60's) where she is beyond her childbearing years. Abram deals directly with God over this in Genesis 15, partly leading to the reiteration of the covenant quoted above. In Gen 15:4, God promises Abram that the heir will be of his own flesh and blood. God again refers to Abram's offspring in Genesis 13:16, 15:4, 17:16-19, and 17:21 in addition to other places where He refers to Abram's descendants.

Famine

After a period of time, the length of which is not specifically referenced in the Bible, we know there was a famine in the land in which Abram and his family resided. A famine, of course, would be a concern to anyone responsible for a family or group of people. We know from Genesis 12:10 that this prompted Abram to travel to Egypt. Examining Abram's move to Egypt, an observation/question is presented by David Guzik, pastor of Calvary Chapel in Santa Barbara, California in his study of this passage[10]:

a. There was a famine in the land: Abram was not wrong for being concerned about famine and feeding his family, but Abram was wrong in thinking God would not provide for his needs in the place where God called him to live. After all, God called Abram to Canaan, not to Egypt.

i. *Abram, like most of us, found it easier to trust God in the far-off promises than in the right-now needs.*

b. Abraham went down to Egypt: When we are tested in this way, we often believe our actions are all right because no harm can come. Though God blessed and protected Abram even in Egypt, he came away with excess baggage and a rebuke from a pagan king. Harm came.

i. *The harm especially shows up later when a slave girl named Hagar - whom Sarai received when in Egypt - is a source of great trouble to this family.*

I bring this up for a good reason. Although I am in no way as learned or scholarly as David Guzik, a man for whom I have the utmost respect, I disagree with the parts of this submission that infer Abram was wrong to go to Egypt, a position others have stated to me in discussions for similar reasons.

I believe that God intended for Abram to go to Egypt as part of His declaration of Himself. Had Abram not gone to Egypt, we would not have had the deception or interaction with Pharaoh. Had we not had Pharaoh with the need to be in God's good graces, he would not have presented Hagar to Sarai as a servant. Had Hagar not come to Sarai as a servant, Ishmael would not have been born and we would not have the demonstration of courage and faith that Hagar will give us. We would also not have the lessons about faith derived from the actions and experiences of Sarai. As we have a fair amount of certainty that Hagar was also Keturah, Abram would not have had Keturah/Hagar as a wife after Sarah died. For my Muslim readers, you will certainly recognise the repercussions for Islam had Ishmael not been born. For these reasons, I do believe that Abram's move to Egypt was indeed divinely inspired and that he should not be thought less of for making this decision.

Deception

In Genesis 12:11-13, we come to the deception that begins the chain of events that give us the story of Hagar.

In these verses, as Abram and his entourage are travelling in Egypt, we learn that Abram is afraid that once the Egyptians see his wife's beauty, he will be killed. If Abram were to be killed, his wife would be eligible to become an Egyptian's wife or perhaps, simply be taken as a concubine. Abram tells Sarai that if she and he call each other brother and sister, then his life will be spared and he will be treated well because of her beauty. I should point out that Abraham created this deception again with King Abimelek in Genesis 20. As if that isn't enough, Abraham's son Isaac, with his wife Rebekah, pulled a very similar deception in Genesis 26: 7-10 on the same King Abimelek, king of the Philistines.

From my own Bible study and reflection, I tie these examples of deception to an important lesson. Deception (lies) will always be found out. These weren't little white lies either, these were elaborate deceptions that would have had to involve a significant number of Abram's household. In all of these instances, the deceptions were uncovered with varying repercussions. Fortunately, they were mostly positive. I don't think that in today's day and age he would be sent on our way with a handmaid or gifts. The lesson, however, is there to learn.

The key factor in this deception played upon Pharaoh, is what happened between Pharaoh and Sarai before the deception was uncovered. Specifically, Genesis 12:15, where so few words say so many things: *"And when Pharaoh's officials saw her, they praised her to Pharaoh, and she was taken into his palace."* When we combine this with verse 17, *"But the Lord inflicted serious diseases on Pharaoh and his household because of Abram's wife Sarai"*, we get a very clear picture that Pharaoh quite likely took Sarai to his bed — in the Biblical sense. Conversely, the previously quoted Sahih Bukhari (Vol 4, Book 55) Hadith 578 says that *"the infidel's plot was foiled"*, indicating that Sarai was not taken to Pharaoh's bed.

Regardless, our story now starts to get some legs. Because of this deception, because Pharaoh sinned in the eyes of God, God inflicted serious diseases on Pharaoh and his household. This was the catalyst for both the expulsion of Abram from Egypt and the gift to Sarai (thus Abram) of the woman we know as Hagar — the woman who would become a servant in Abram's household.

We have to ask ourselves a couple of contentious questions here. If Abram had gone to Egypt and carried out this deception without God's inspiration, why was only Pharaoh punished? Why was Sarai not punished as well? If God did inspire this move and the events that followed, why should He punish Pharaoh? Whether God inspired these events or not is a question I cannot answer. I know that I believe God inspired them, but I am not learned enough to state that equivocally. What I can state equivocally, however, was that this entire situation gave God the opportunity to demonstrate his love for Abram and his love for Sarai and the lengths that He would go to protect them. With his infliction of punishment on Pharaoh, God is basically saying, "I AM", something God will state outright in Exodus 3. Starting in Exodus 7, we read quite plainly in the story of the ten plagues that God hardens Pharaoh's heart (a different Pharaoh) against Israel so that He may demonstrate his power so that *the Egyptians will know that I am the Lord..."* (Ex 7:5).

> *"For my thoughts are not your thoughts, neither are your ways my ways," declares the Lord. "As the heavens are higher than the earth, so are my ways higher than your ways and my thoughts than your thoughts." (Isaiah 55:8-9)*

I think that Isaiah 55:8-9 teaches us an important lesson about these questions. It is not for us to know or understand the mind of God. We must, however, trust that what God does is right because, well, He's God! It's not asking the question that is the problem (read the first few chapters of Job), but it is denying God's right or altogether dismissing God or dismissing God's omniscience by the results of the question that becomes the problem.

In the time of Abram, the land was full of many pagan religions and many pagan gods. The ORACC project list hosted by the University of Pennsylvania lists over 40 pagan deities in ancient Mesopotamian culture in their *Ancient Mesopotamian Gods and Goddesses* project[11]. Mesopotamia, which is modern day Syria and Iraq, is North and East of Egypt, and east of Canaan. I think all readers will recognise from our own grade school studies that Egypt was ripe with gods for this, gods for that, and gods for the other. To the Egyptians, the God of Abram was initially just another one of the same (Ex. 8:25). While God was heavily present in the lives of those within the lineage of Abram, there was a whole world full of people that had not yet been exposed to His presence. This meant that God's love and grace would get lost quite fast in the praising, idolatry, and fear mongering of the pagan deity adherents that were prevalent.

It's for these reasons I believe that it was necessary for God to demonstrate his power and thus demonstrate his love. It is for these reasons throughout the Pentateuch and beyond that made it necessary for God to create situations where His power and love would shine because of their reality, over the empty promises of the pagan deities that couldn't do anything, because they weren't real.

While I find it unfortunate to be able to do this, I have to draw a parallel to the modern world. God had to market himself. God had to sell himself to those he wanted to follow Him. God had to demonstrate His power and omniscience in a world of competing products (pagan deities). I don't mean that in crass terms and certainly don't mean it disrespectfully. I mean the reality of the day was that it was a necessity that God had to create situations where He would be able to demonstrate his power, love, and primacy. He had to demonstrate the truth in the advertising, if you will allow another mundane comparison. In other words, "God declares Himself".

While I may have been a bit long winded on this topic, there is a reason for it. We now have a fuller perspective to carry with us as we read about the woman whom God put in a difficult situation and then when she tried to escape, asked her to go back to it. There were things to be accomplished, and she was part of His plan.

Chapter 5

Understanding Loss of Control

It is important to understand that when I speak of "loss of control" I am not speaking about a lack of willpower or a lack of self-control. I am speaking about forces in our life orchestrated by events and people beyond the scope or reach of our ability to counteract easily.

There are experiences, emotional experiences, that we all share and some of them we share to greater degrees. The sense of a loss of control is something we have all encountered in our life, repeatedly. Understanding that feeling of loss of control is vital to understanding the story of Hagar.

> "So far, the most important lesson I have learned is, that at this point in my life, it is better to shake loose that idea of having 100% control. When I try to plan my life, it never goes the way I expect and that often leaves me stressed, disappointed or frustrated." Molly Mahar ~ www.stratejoy.com

Have you ever felt swept along by events, out of control, at the mercy and whim of others? No matter how much control we have over our lives, there is always someone we answer to. This can be a microcosmic slice of life, or it can be the macrocosm of our existence.

In the microcosm, we can be swept out of control within the family unit, in the workplace, or perhaps in a social structure. In the macrocosm, our existence is controlled right up the pillar of responsibility to the Prime Minister. Some would argue that the top dog of the land is actually the Supreme Court, who can exercise power over the Prime Minister. For many of us, the buck stops with God. However, given the nearly globalised separation of Church and State, that's two different pillars of responsibility we are subject to (state and church), although I would agree there is a necessary blending at points within those two pillars.

These two prominent pillars of responsibility don't always see things the same way either, thus causing other situations where we get swept along, against our own judgement. Taking a step back and putting a biblical spin on this topic, we could say that the two pillars of responsibility in our lives are the Pillar of the Mundane and the Pillar of Grace (what we do in life and what we believe in life).

When we were children, having others in finite control of our lives was a matter of course, thankfully. At very young ages we certainly did not know enough about life or ourselves to be the ones at the helm. At some point in our childhood progression through life, we do begin to take responsibility for ourselves. Good parenting, good community, good role models all help us strive to become more and will give us the opportunities to learn and experience responsibility first hand. Through late grade school and into junior high school we start taking on more and more responsibilities. These can be personal responsibilities, familial responsibilities, or cultural responsibilities (friends, organisations, the church, the community). By the time we get to high school, we are pretty well self-sufficient and self-actualizing in many regards. Our parents can usually rely on us to complete tasks, follow the rules (at least the ones that we don't think are totally stupid), and generally not burn the house down on a relatively frequent basis. If we remember back to our earlier years with clarity, some of the most frustrating moments occurred when things didn't "go our way" or more pointedly, when we held no sway over the currents we were floundering in.

As high school ends and new experiences arise for us, the blossom into adulthood arrives. This brings more responsibility in the two pillars. At some point we meet the person of our dreams, fall madly in love, and then start living as our own new family unit. We take on the responsibility to a certain extent for each other, and certainly we take on the responsibility to the new family unit. Then, with luck, God blesses us with the responsibility of parenthood. Our own little ankle-biters start growing up. We watch them start to learn about responsibility, and we see the circle completed … or more accurately, starting over again. Only now it's our turn to lead, our turn to be the one wielding the control.

We have much in our lives that we have to be responsible for. We have many micro-goals and waypoints to reach. It's no wonder then that when something or someone steps in and takes hold of the helm that we can get so upset or in some situations, be relieved. Usually, it's "the man" that we find ourselves railing against in the form of some law, legislation, or rule that prevents us from doing what we want to do.

A new boss with a different vision than what you are used to can certainly upset the apple cart. A playground or workplace bully can be particularly frustrating. Getting pulled over by a police officer when you just *have* to get to the doctor's appointment can be a few minutes of resentment mixed within the hectic hours of our day. Watch how fast a person can go from calm to crazy with an obstinate and unrelenting child in a state of defiance. Perish forbid more serious control isn't seized from us, such as when one is facing criminal charges, incarceration, or an invading army. The frustration and queasiness we sometimes feel when things go out of our control can even be brought on by simpler things, like a car that won't start, an overdrawn chequing account, or by finding a car parked across the entrance to our driveway.

The stronger, more self-sufficient, and more independent you are to begin with, the greater the impact that these events and situations can have on you. The more you are used to feeling in control of the situations and events in your life, the stronger you feel the frustration and helplessness when that control is taken away or interfered with. The more you have control taken away from you in your life, the more sensitive you become to it happening in the future.

I think that our perspectives on the subject of control being wrested away from us may be widened by having the experiences of those from other lands to compare our days to. Of course, having the perspective of the experiences of those from other times would be even more eye-opening. For the discussion in this book, it's important that you have the perspective and understanding of the feeling of control being taken from you to properly appreciate and understand the woman we are looking at. I hope I've conveyed those feelings of being out of control so that you can have a deeper understanding of Hagar's challenges as we delve into her story.

Another frustration we are going to find in the life of Hagar is persecution at the hands of another, simply for who she is. Modern day Christians should have a perspective of persecution as Christian martyrdom is alive and well in this day and age, as it was in the years following our Lord's blood sacrifice. A visit to *Voice of the Martyr* (www.persecution.com) will tell countless stories of modern day followers of our Lord Jesus Christ who have had all control taken away from them at the hands of unbelievers. Our friends in Israel live in a hot zone of persecution. Our friends at the local mosque will also be well aware of this feeling. The Shia have been subjected to persecution by the Sunni since 632 AD.

Hagar's story is retold day-to-day in our post-modern world.

Strength

Strength can appear in many forms, and in many circumstances.

"The wailing and crying that comes from the depths of your soul," she recalled to ABC News last year. "The pain is so horrible."[12]

These were the words of Renee Napier, recalling what it was like after learning that her 20-year-old daughter Meagan and her friend Lisa had been instantly killed by a drunk driver on May 11th, 2002. A decade later, Renee Napier, joined by the man that killed her daughter and her daughter's friend, are national speakers for the prevention of DUI[13]. Choosing forgiveness over hatred, Renee shares the stage with the convicted felon that killed the two young girls. This kind of forgiveness[14] is one that can only come from a deep well of strength.

Faith

An example of faith by a single mother can be found in this one[15]:

I thought marriage would heal the disappointment and doubt that plagued my adolescent years. When it didn't, I turned to heavy bouts of drinking. After years of wallowing in my own self-pity and loathing, I sought counseling and worked on co-dependency, anger issues, and self-esteem. At the same time, I also quit drinking! Finally, I began to face my future with determination.

However, when my therapist recommended that my husband and I seek marriage counseling, my husband was not interested. His response was "If you're not happy, then you know where the door is." At that point I knew that our journey together had ended.

With a six-year-old son and a two-year-old daughter by my side, I returned to Pennsylvania, where I grew up. With my mother's support, I became a stay-at-home working mom and built a successful home-based business.

It wasn't easy. We lived in a seventy-two foot, single wide trailer. Meals consisted of TV dinners or macaroni and cheese, and child support was very sporadic. In addition, we incurred the extra expense of being in and out of the courts over a period of many years.

However, our sense of peace and love for one another made those times more than worth it! Eighteen years later I'm still single, still sober, and have a successful business. Through God's faithfulness and grace, we not only survived, but we thrived. If I can do it by the grace of God, so can you. There is joy in the journey, and life is good!

Courage

A single dad's courage to do what he must is an example for us as well[16]:

When my son was nine months, she bought a ticket back to China and left us. Nobody knows what I've been through, it was hell. I've had a rough ride. I was working full-time for the NHS and explained to my line manager that I needed to cut my hours. But she was abrupt and unsympathetic. I was leaving work, rushing to pick up my son and daughter, give them their tea, they were tired and stressed, so was I. Also, my son got very ill, he was affected by breastfeeding stopping suddenly.

Eventually, I took early retirement from my job, I set up an electronic engineering business but again found it too much combining work and kids. Now I'm on income support and will be until my son starts school. It's the first time I've ever lived on benefits.

I try to blend in but I am unusual, being a single dad in a small village. I sympathise with other single parents, keep your chin up, I say. I don't have any family around me to help. But by now I'm used to pulling my socks up and getting on with it, so that's what I do.

Afternoon movies and Harlequin romance novels could make a fortune on the events of Hagar's story. This doesn't diminish the value of the story but illustrates its timelessness and potency. As you read these pages, put yourself in Hagar's place to try and understand her, to try and fully appreciate who she was and what she lived through. This will make the woman's strength, courage, and faith (trust) in God an even more powerful experience for you.

Chapter 6
Understanding Hagar's Story

While it is unclear exactly when Abram entered Egypt, date wise, we know it was some period before 1920 BCE (2084 AM) according to the *Annals of the World*[17]. Based on the events in Egypt (Genesis 12) we can guess that it was only a short amount of time before this. While entering Egypt, there was an interesting event that took place with Abram and Sarai (Genesis 12:10-20), one to be repeated by Abram (Genesis 20:2) and his son Isaac (Genesis 26:7). As Abram was afraid that he would be killed when the men of the land (Egypt) looked upon the beauty of his wife Sarai, Abram lied and claimed Sarai was his sister. Because, through deception, she was thought only to be Abram's sister and was very fair, she was *"taken into Pharaoh's house"* (Genesis 12:15). Of course, Abram was very well treated and enriched due to the Pharaoh's interest in Abram's "sister". Sarai obviously played along and played the role given to her. As a result of this deception, as discussed previously, Pharaoh expelled them from Egypt (Genesis 12:18-20).

To atone for his sin, or perhaps simply to appease the God of Abram, Pharaoh gave a very valuable gift to Sarai. He gave her a maidservant, his own daughter. She became an integral part of Abram's household.

It is reported in the Genesis Rabbah 45:1 that Hagar was the daughter of Pharaoh. The Pharaoh, who I believe was Amenemhat II, seeing what great miracles God had done for Sarai's sake, said, "It is better for Hagar to be a slave in Sarai's house than mistress in her own."

The Reality of Pharaoh's Decision

In giving his daughter Hagar to Sarai as a servant, the Pharaoh reduced her from high-born princess of the house of Pharaoh to the house of a nomadic tent dweller. This in itself should demonstrate the fear Pharaoh had for the God of Abraham.

Reducing his daughter to this status would have been quite a change for Hagar. Since Egyptians considered the Pharaoh a god incarnate, Pharaoh's decision would also have been without question for her, even though women of the household held a place equal to men in Egyptian society. This isn't to say she was equal to Pharaoh, merely to illustrate the difference between the culture of Egypt and the nomadic culture of Abram.

"The ancient Hebrew family was patriarchal by nature. The Hebrew term to describe it was beth'ab, the "house of one's father." The father was the supreme authority over the family. When his children grew older and his sons married, they and their children came also under his control. If he had more than one wife or if the children were the offspring of concubines or servants, these all assumed a position on a common basis with his other children. Thus, the sons of Jacob by four different mothers were all accepted on equal terms. The family also included those of no blood kin who had entered into a covenant relationship, not to mention servants and retainers."[18]

The Hebrew family was patriarchal. The man of the house was the master of his wife and possessed absolute authority over his children, including the power of life and death. As the wife of a rich man, Sarai would have had her own handmaids and servants. She would have been fed, wined, and entertained. Her clothing would have been the finest and her lifestyle one that would be quite different to that of a city dweller. That's not to say it wasn't a hard life, but within the scope of the life they had, as the Patriarch's wife, it would have been a good life.

This part of the back story has to give us pause for reflection. The daughter of Pharaoh, the daughter of the ruler of Egypt, the daughter of a king and in the beliefs of the day, the daughter of a god is given to servitude. The high-born and high-placed young woman was taken from her life of Egyptian luxury and sent to a nomadic existence, walking the desert and living in tents (albeit, very nice tents) as a servant to others. She would be the one bringing the towels, not having the towels brought to her. She would be the one having to clean up after others, not having others clean up after her. While her mistress would be enjoying the nomadic version of a regal-style life, this Egyptian princess would be standing humbly at the side of the room waiting to be beckoned to serve her "betters".

Concubine or Wife?

We can gain a better understanding of Hagar's role and position by looking at the original Hebrew text. The author could have referred to her as an *abuddah*[19], the term for another's piece of property or a slave. However, that was not the term used, so thinking of Hagar as a piece of property or a slave is incorrect. The term applied to Hagar in Genesis 1:1 is *shiphchah*. While in later times this term came to mean roughly the same as *abuddah,* at the time of this story the term *shiphchah* is best understood by looking at the Ugaritic verb form of the word meaning "being together", which is closely related to the Hebrew word for "clan"[20]. In this context, *shiphchah* is referring to[18]:

> "… someone who joins or is attached to a person or a clan. If Hagar was a gift to Sarai from Pharaoh, this interpretation would be the best fit."

While Pharaoh would have been an absolute ruler and his decree would be an absolute law for his daughter, you have to wonder what this did to the woman emotionally. She was being told that living a life of servitude (at any level) to a bunch of nomadic tent dwellers was better than a life of luxury in the palaces of Egypt, with her family; all because her father couldn't keep it in his pants. From the Biblical story, we know that Pharaoh would have made this decision because of his recognition of the power and supremacy of Abram's God. At this point, Hagar would not have had the opportunity to see His works or power.

42

Imagine how you would have felt as a teenager if your parents had literally given you to a band of gypsies, totally removed from your family, your friends, and all that you knew, for you to be an unpaid servant for the rest of your life.

Of course, there is the argument that Hagar was a concubine because Abram went "in unto her". In the context of the culture of the day, if a man engaged in coitus with a woman in the privacy of his home (without witnesses), then they were married[21]. Therefore, there are some writings that reference her as a wife. However, they may be confusing the fact that Abram married Keturah after the death of Sarah, and Keturah has been identified as Hagar (as already mentioned), returned from Paran.

Many adherents of Islam assert that she was indeed Abram's wife[22]:

> "Some Muslims claim she had the status of a legal wife because they seemingly think the status of Hagar has implications for the status of Ishmael and hence for the question whether the Arabs and in particular Muhammad are rightfully part of the covenant God made with Abraham, and whether Muhammad is qualified to be a prophet under the promises of God."

However, even though the translations in the KJV and the NIV say that Sarai gave Hagar to Abram to be his wife, looking at the original Hebrew text gives us more insight. The original Hebrew translates literally as, "Abram • woman of • Sarai • and she is taking."[37]

The Hebrew word *ishshah* (H802) literally translated as "woman-of" is the feminine form of two other

43

Hebrew words: *iysh* (H376) which means man, and *enowsh* (H582) which means mortal. *Ishshah* is also a Hebrew word used for wife; there are eleven Hebrew words that can be interpreted as wife. A Karaite translator, Yochanan Zaqantov, gives the following contextual translation and explanation[23]:

> "So Sarai, Abram's wife (*eshet*), took her maid, Hagar the Egyptian—after Abram had dwelt in the land of Canaan ten years—and gave her to her husband (*iyshah*) Abram as concubine.

> The difference in pronunciation is very similar to Ishah (Alpeh-Sin-Hey) and Iysh'ah (Aleph-Yod-Shin-Hey). The first way is of the woman and the second way is the making of Ish (Aleph-Yod-Shin) as denoting a feminine usage by adding the hey ending or belonging to the woman. Literally speaking "Her man" is what it is saying.

> If we fully transliterate we can see the relationship. So, the reason we are focusing on the belonging to one another is that it means they are in a relationship."

With this explanation, the point is being made that *Iysh* (man/husband) is to *Ishah* (woman/wife), as *Iyshah* (her man/husband) is to *Ish'to* (his woman/wife). So, was Hagar Abram's wife? It doesn't really matter. What matters is that she bore Ishmael, Abram's first child.

Setting the Stage

Now we move forward a bit in time. We have left Egypt and are now in the land of Canaan. Abram and

44

his nephew Lot had recently parted ways in Canaan (Genesis 13:5-12), in the land between Bethel and Hai. Abram and Lot and their families had grown to such size that the land they were on would not support both of them (Genesis 13:6). Adding to the troubles of the day, Abram and Lot weren't getting along that well. The next verse (Genesis 13:7) refers to strife between the two great men's herdsmen. Making a break from things, Lot dwells in Jordan (Genesis 13:11) while Abram remains in Canaan. It is here that God furthers His covenant with Abram (Genesis 13:14-17), the covenant which is, in effect, giving the Promised Land to Abram's descendants.

Abram moves on and settles on the Plains of Mamre, near Hebron in 1920 BCE (2084 AM)[16]. These were indeed troubling times for Abram and would have provided a backdrop of uncertainty for all of his family and retinue, including Hagar. This was not a peaceful land. It was during this period leading up to our story that Chedorlaomer, king of Elam, led the siege on Sodom and Gomorrah (Genesis 14), taking Abram's nephew Lot as a captive. Shortly on the heels of this, Abram led the slaughter of Chedorlaomer and his cohorts to rescue Lot and his family. A relatively short period of time later, the Lord rained down destruction on the cities of Sodom and Gomorrah (Genesis 19).

Living as a princess in Egypt, Hagar would have been far removed from battle and strife, nestled safely in the walls of Pharaoh's palace. Living with the tent dwellers in the desert, however, she was living close to the front lines and would have had no illusion of the safety she now lacked and that Pharaoh no longer offered her.

An Error in Judgement

While Abram had a very great tribe, he and his wife Sarai were, as I have said, childless. Though the Lord promised Abram an heir of his own flesh (Genesis 15:4), Sarai had some doubt about this. This was because Abram was roughly eighty years old and his wife Sarai was only ten years younger. The confusing part of this for the couple was the promises made that Abram would have an heir of his own flesh and blood and that his descendants would be innumerable. These promises did not align with the couple's age and reproductive status.

The story of Hagar begins in earnest when Sarai makes an error in judgement (or was it unknowingly divinely compelled?). She believes that she has to fulfil God's promise, rather than have faith that God would fulfil the promise as stated. The story starts in Genesis 16:1-4:

> *"Now Sarai, Abram's wife, had borne him no children. But she had an Egyptian slave named Hagar; so she said to Abram, "The Lord has kept me from having children. Go, sleep with my slave; perhaps I can build a family through her." Abram agreed to what Sarai said. So after Abram had been living in Canaan ten years, Sarai his wife took her Egyptian slave Hagar and gave her to her husband to be his wife. He slept with Hagar, and she conceived. When she knew she was pregnant, she began to despise her mistress."*

It was not an uncommon practice at this time that a woman, who was barren, could find another woman for her husband to have a child with. This would have been an acceptable practice under Mesopotamian Law. As this story transpires less than two hundred years before the Code of Hammurabi, we don't know for sure if Sumerian, Assyrian, or Babylonian laws would have applied to Abram and his family. However, the Code of Hammurabi being so highly respected, we can assume that it would be very similar to whatever laws would have applied to Abram and his family. While we do not have exact text to this law in the earliest records of Mesopotamian Law available (2112 BCE to 2095 BCE)[24], the oldest, almost fully intact set of laws discovered so far is The Code of Hammurabi (Hammurabi reigned 1795 to 1750 BCE) which gives us the law that would have applied to this situation. This narrative deals with laws 144 through 146 of the Code[25], the laws of Abram's society would have been similar or at least closely representative for this time period:

> Monogamy was the rule, and a childless wife might give her husband a maid (who was no wife) to bear him children, who were reckoned hers. She remained mistress of her maid, but Sarai could not sell Hagar if she had borne her husband children. If the wife did this, the Code did not allow the husband to take a concubine. If she would not, he could do so. The concubine was a wife, though not of the same rank; the first wife had no power over her. A concubine was a free woman, was often dowered for marriage and her children were legitimate. She could only be divorced on the same

conditions as a wife. If a wife became a chronic invalid, the husband was bound to maintain her in the home they had made together, unless she preferred to take her dowry and go back to her father's house; but he was free to remarry. In all these cases the children were legitimate and legal heirs.

There was, of course, no hindrance to a man having children by a slave or servant. These children were free, in any case, and their mother could not be sold, though she might be pledged, and she was free on her master's death. These children could be legitimized by their father's acknowledgment before witnesses, and were often adopted. They then ranked equally in sharing their father's estate, but if not adopted, the wife's children divided and took first choice."

Old Testament Polygamy

We know that marriages with multiple wives were not unheard of in the Pentateuch. Polygamous marriage was first seen with Lamech around 3130 BCE (930 AM). Lamech took two wives, Adah and Zillah. I should point out that the Lamech mentioned is a descendant of Cain (Genesis 4:17-18) and not Lamech who was the father of Noah, who were descendants of Adam and Eve's third son, Seth (Genesis 5:3-29, 1 Chronicles 1:1-4).

We also find polygamy referenced in Mosaic Law, in Deuteronomy 21:15 we read:

"If a man has two wives, one loved and the other unloved ..."

There are, however, circumstances that would have caused God to overlook it, for a greater good. There are approximately the same number of men and women in the world as of 2015 (50.5% men, 49.5% women)[26]. It wouldn't be too much of a stretch to say the birthrate in ancient times would have been proportionately similar, though I have not been able to reference this. Regardless of the exact proportions and aside from the birthrates by gender, it was a patriarchal society, which inherently meant there would be fewer adult men regardless of the birth rate. It was the men out in the fields who would die by accident or by overwork. It was the men who went to war and reading through the Pentateuch, there was more than enough war to go around. There would have definitely been a surplus on the feminine side of the equation. Women who could not get a husband and had no family would be reduced to death by starvation or suicide, a life of prostitution or slavery. In addition to the need to look after the women, it would enable a much faster expansion of humanity. At this point in the history, the population of the world was relatively low and they needed to procreate abundantly. God did not tell people to be polygamous. It was something they chose to do to address a societal problem and a population problem. While God's original plan was one woman, one man, this was a societal issue and not a spiritual/faith/worship problem.

Pentecostal minister Don Stewart offered this commentary on the reasons for polygamy being practised[27]:

> The practice of a man marrying more than one wife was common in the ancient world. There are a number of reasons why this was so. They include the following:
>
> 1. There were more females than males.
> 2. There was a desire to increase the wealth of the household.
> 3. A large number of children was needed to work the fields or with the herds.
> 4. Many females died in childbirth.
> 5. In nomadic communities it was important for every female to be attached to a household.

Monsignor Charles Pope, a dean and pastor in the Archdiocese of Washington, DC, writes the following about polygamy in the Bible[28]:

> "It is also clear that the customs of the ancient Near East also infected Israel's notion of marriage and that many, at least wealthier men and patriarchs, did often take more than one wife. Thus, we see that sin corrupted what God intended and that, for a time, God overlooked this sinful behavior.
>
> However, we ought not equate the mere reporting of sinful behavior with approval of it. For, while the polygamy of the patriarchs is reported, so is all the trouble it caused wherein brothers of different mothers contended and even killed one another.

For example, there are terrible stories told of the sons of Gideon, and also the sons of Jacob, to mention but two. The well-known story of Joseph being sold into slavery by his brothers emerges from the internecine conflicts of brothers of different mothers. Hence while reporting polygamy, the Bible also teaches of the evil it brings forth.

Gradually God led the ancient Jews from approving of polygamy such that, by the time of Jesus, it was rare."

On the website answersingenesis.org, author Roger Patterson writes[29]:

"After the Flood, there are many mentions of polygamous relationships—including among the patriarchs of Israel. Abraham, Jacob, David, and Solomon all had multiple wives. It is interesting to note that there are no passages in Scripture that clearly state, "No man should have more than one wife." However, polygamous relationships are never mentioned in a positive light, and, indeed, the problems of such relationships are presented.

Consider the consequences revealed in Scripture in each of the following cases: Abraham—led to bitterness between Sarah and her maid, Hagar, and the eventual dismissal of Hagar and Ishmael; Jacob—led to Rachel's jealousy of Leah and to Joseph being betrayed and sold by his half-brothers; David—led to the rape of one of his daughters (Tamar) by one of his sons (Tamar's half-brother Amnon) and Amnon's subsequent murder by Tamar's brother Absalom; Solomon—

his many wives "turned away his heart" from the Lord and to the worship of false gods (1 Kings 11:1–8). Just because the Bible records polygamous relationships does not mean that God approves of such things.

The only direct command against polygamy is given to the kings that were to rule Israel, as they are told not to "multiply wives" to themselves (Deuteronomy 17:17). It is also interesting to note that polygamous relationships seem to be regulated in the commands Moses gave to the nation of Israel. Leviticus 18:18 instructs that a man should not marry sisters, and Deuteronomy 21:15 talks of assigning an heir to a man with two wives. Many commentators suggest that the passages do not endorse polygamy but rather prohibit it. Deuteronomy 21:15 may also be translated as "has had two wives" in succession rather than at the same time. The sisters in Leviticus 18:18 are understood by some to be any Israelite women. Regardless of the interpretation of these passages, the taking of multiple wives is not in accord with God's design from the beginning."

I think it's clear that polygamy was not God's intention for man, but it was practised regardless. We are all, even the patriarchs, sinners.

However, all of that being said, we can gain a better understanding of Hagar's role and position by looking at the original Hebrew text. The author could have referred to her as an *abuddah*[30], the term for another's piece of property or a slave. However, that was not the term so thinking of Hagar as a piece of property of a slave is erroneous. The term applied to Hagar in

Genesis 1:1 is *shiphchah*. While in later times this term came to mean roughly the same as *abuddah,* at the time of this story the term *shiphchah* is best understood by looking at the Ugaritic verb form of the word meaning "being together", which is closely related to the Hebrew word for "clan"[31]. In this context, *shiphchah* is referring to[29]:

"… someone who joins or is attached to a person or a clan. If Hagar was a gift to Sarai from Pharaoh, this interpretation would be the best fit."

Years had passed since God's promise to Abram that he would have a child by Sarai. Ten years had passed since arriving in Canaan. Because Sarai was fearful Abram would not have an heir of his own flesh (Genesis 16:1-2), Sarai took it upon herself to offer a handmaid to Abram to have a child with. This demonstrates a lack of faith in God's word on Sarai's part (another book in its own right).

Sarai and Hagar

Our story officially starts nine years after arriving at the Plain of Mamre, after parting ways from Abram's nephew Lot. Hagar is introduced as an Egyptian handmaid of Sarai (Genesis 16:1) when Sarai gives her to her husband, and her husband accepts. Hagar, being of noble ancestry and birth would have been Sarai's first choice of any maidservant around her. The inherent nobility of Hagar and her selection to be with Abram allows us to infer that up to this point, Hagar and Sarai were on good terms, or were at least cordial. In Genesis 16:4

we are told that after she became pregnant by Abram, Hagar:

> *"... began to despise her mistress. Then Sarai said to Abram, "You are responsible for the wrong I am suffering. I put my slave in your arms, and now that she knows she is pregnant, she despises me. May the Lord judge between you and me."*

There was at least a level of respect between them, as much respect as a rich man's wife would have been able to have for a maidservant, regardless of her status denoted from the use of the word *shiphchah*. Remember, Hagar came to this family after Pharaoh had, though under a cloud of deception, taken Sarai into his house (his bed). That situation would always have coloured any relationship that would have existed between Sarai and Hagar and they both would have been very aware of it. I would argue that at some level, Hagar held a deep resentment and blamed Abram for her position in the household, but there is really nothing I have found that would evidence such a position.

As I illustrated previously, this whole situation presented a very peculiar circumstance. Hagar, a handmaid, yet herself of high birth, was in a position to demand respect by virtue of her birthright. Contrarily, she was required to follow the orders of her mistress, Sarai.

Returning to the story, Sarai gives Hagar to Abram, Abram agrees and "goes in unto her". Hagar conceives right away. The shoe drops.

"And he went in unto Hagar, and she conceived: and when she saw that she had conceived, her mistress was despised in her eyes." (Genesis 16:4)

Hagar's attitude immediately changes towards Sarai. To put it delicately, Hagar becomes a handful. She acts superciliously to her and according to Rabbinical commentary, starts bad mouthing Sarai to those who would listen[32]:

> "Referring to the report that when she had conceived she began to despise her mistress, the Rabbis say that she gossiped about Sarah, saying: "She is certainly not as godly as she pretends to be, for in all the years of her married life she has had no children, while I conceived at once" (Gen. R. xlv.; Sefer ha-Yashar, Lek Leka). Sarah took revenge (Gen. xvi.) by preventing her intercourse with Abraham, by whipping her with her slipper, and by exacting humiliating services, such as carrying her bathing-materials to the bath (l.c.); she further caused Hagar by an evil eye to miscarry, and Ishmael, therefore, was her second child, as is inferred from the fact that the angel prophesied that she would bear a child (Gen. xvi. 11), while it had been narrated before that she was pregnant (Gen. xvi. 4)"

While the circumstances may have become difficult for Sarai, they became downright horrible for Hagar. The fears and nightmares about her situation that she would undoubtedly have entertained were now coming true. Hagar would have faced an emotional wall that would have been equally as insurmountable to a woman of today's era in a similar, horrid, situation.

"And Sarai said unto Abram, My wrong be upon thee: I have given my maid into thy bosom; and when she saw that she had conceived, I was despised in her eyes: the Lord judge between me and thee. But Abram said unto Sarai, Behold, thy maid is in thy hand; do to her as it pleaseth thee. And when Sarai dealt hardly with her, she fled from her face." (Genesis 16:5-6)

Sarai's treatment of Hagar, after the forced conception, became so horrid and unbearable that Hagar flees to the wilderness (Genesis 16:6). To put this in perspective, Hagar would have grown up as an Egyptian Princess well aware of a maidservant's place in the hierarchy of the household. A princess of the Pharaoh was a daughter of Egypt because her father, the Pharaoh, *was* Egypt. She would have been well aware of the concept of servitude, what it meant, and what the rules of behaviour were for her. She would also have been well aware of what the punishment for her would be in the circumstances of rebellion or abandonment of her post. She had been living this life, in this position, for ten years as our story progresses. Hagar would have thought that she had a modicum of safety from the fact she was carrying Abram's child, but that would only have bought her life, not bought her absolution from further punishment. Hagar flees to the wilderness and heads towards Shur (suggested to have been located on the eastern side of the head of the Red Sea[33]).

The First Christophany - A Pivotal Encounter For All People of Faith

We are now entering a powerful and important part of this story of Hagar. The message here must not be lost to a misunderstanding of what you are reading. It contains a message so powerful as to, in my humble opinion, overshadow all of the rest of the story of Hagar. I'll reveal this and examine it as we continue.

Fleeing to this particular wilderness would also have been an act of desperation as well. Remember, the Plains of Mamre are a land of desert and scrub brush. Food, shelter, and safety would all have been scarcely available under the best of circumstances, but to a pregnant woman fleeing without the protection of a master, they would have been almost impossible to attain. To flee to the desert in such an isolated and harsh place would have been a self-imposed death sentence. Again, from her desperate act, we can further deduce the untenable nature of her situation under the angry and embittered hand of Sarai.

> *"And the angel of the Lord found her by a fountain of water in the wilderness, by the fountain in the way to Shur. And he said, Hagar, Sarai's maid, whence camest thou? and whither wilt thou go? And she said, I flee from the face of my mistress Sarai. And the angel of the Lord said unto her, Return to thy mistress, and submit thyself under her hands. And the angel of the Lord said unto her, I will multiply thy seed exceedingly, that it shall not be numbered for multitude. And the angel of the Lord said unto her, Behold, thou art with child, and shalt bear a son, and shalt call his name*

Ishmael; because the Lord hath heard thy affliction. And he will be a wild man; his hand will be against every man, and every man's hand against him; and he shall dwell in the presence of all his brethren." (Genesis 21:7-12)

After an unknown length of time that Hagar was in the desert, she is found by an angel of the Lord. He asks her where she is coming from and where she is going. She replies that she is fleeing from her mistress Sarai. As this is the angel of the Lord, it may seem silly that he asked her these things. Shouldn't the angel already know them? This is something that we frequently see in the Bible.

If we go back to the garden of Eden, we see God asking Adam in Genesis 3:9, *"Where art thou?"* Again, in Genesis 3:11 God asks, *"Who told thee that thou wast naked? Hast thou eaten of the tree, whereof I commanded thee that thou shouldest not eat?"* God is all knowing. God is not asking these questions because he doesn't know, of course God already knows. What the Lord is doing by asking these questions of Adam is giving Adam the opportunity to own up to his mistakes, to speak the truth to the Lord, to acknowledge what had been done, to confess his sin. We find a similar situation here. Hagar fled from her master's tent without her master's blessing: she had done wrong. The angel is giving her the opportunity to be truthful and to acknowledge her mistake, to confess, which she does.

One thing that is very important to understand here is the Christophany; the pre-incarnate appearance of Christ[34]. In Bible study, there is an important concept called the "Principle of First Mention." That is:

"Under the First Mention Principle, the idea is that God indicates the truth that stands in His mind that will not change later on. This means that the initial discussion of any subject in the Bible would have unusual significance by this standard, as Benjamin Willis Newton (a 19th century Plymouth Brethren member) observed."[35]

I believe that the all-important truth that God is revealing to Hagar, a truth that will never be reversed, is the truth of His forgiveness and His compassion.

In Genesis 21:7-12 is the very first appearance of the Angel of the Lord. Paraphrasing Jon Courson[36]:

"It's no ordinary angel, not one of the heavenly multitudes with wings on their backs and a halo over their heads. The angel of the Lord in the OT is a very special messenger; capital "M" Messenger. It's called a Christophany. It's an appearance of Jesus Christ, the second person of the trinity, before he appeared in Bethlehem through the Virgin Mary. When he appears, people bow down and worship him fervently. In scripture, angels refuse to accept worship. Since the Angel of the Lord accepts worship, it shows His deity."

It's important to point out here that not only is the pre-incarnate Jesus appearing to a maidservant fleeing the household to which she belongs, but He is also pointedly *not* appearing first to Abram. Whereas God has appeared to Abram in Genesis 12:7 (theophany), the second aspect of God (second aspect of the New Testament Trinity) is making His first appearance to Hagar. One of the lessons that stand out here is the dichotomy between the master of the household

(Abram) and a maidservant. That God has individually sought out Abram and individually sought out Hagar is an exclamation of God's love for all who would fall between the two opposites. This passage is a declaration of God's love for all, regardless of birth, position or how they see themselves. To put it more simply, using the title of a book by Pope Benedict XVI: *Deus caritas est* (God is love).

To emphasise this, the angel of the Lord makes her a promise:

> *"And the angel of the Lord said unto her, I will multiply thy seed exceedingly, that it shall not be numbered for multitude."*

Hagar is the only woman in the Bible to receive such a promise from God. It is a counterpoint to Sarai's own actions. What Sarai tried to do for herself (create a lineage through Hagar), God is fulfilling his original promise to Abram through Hagar first. This again is an exemplar of placing your trust in God over your own understanding. It brings a few verses to mind:

> *"Do not be anxious about anything, but in every situation, by prayer and petition, with thanksgiving, present your requests to God."* *(Philippians 4:6)*

> *"Keep your lives free from the love of money and be content with what you have, because God has said, "Never will I leave you; never will I forsake you.""* *(Hebrews 13:5)*

> *"Trust in the LORD with all your heart and lean not on your own understanding;"* *(Proverbs 3:5)*

But why does He promise her this? Why does he promise her a multitude of offspring? The answer to that is quite simple. In Genesis 15, God makes a promise to Abram:

> *"He took him outside and said, "Look up at the sky and count the stars—if indeed you can count them." Then he said to him, "So shall your offspring be." (Genesis 15:5)*

By promising Hagar that her seed (Ishmael) would be multiplied is merely a matter of that promise being kept, because Ishmael is the son of Abram.

Not only is the angel of the Lord appearing to a maidservant, but he is also appearing to an Egyptian woman (not a Hebrew) who is running away from her household. Her actions are both illegal and immoral in the context of that culture. She belonged to Abram's household, and by leaving, she would be kidnapping Abram's unborn son whom she carried in her womb. Is the angel of the Lord there to punish her for this transgression? No.

Dr J. Vernon McGee tells us[33], "How gracious God is to her. It's not her sin, so God very graciously deals with her." He goes on to say how overwhelmed she is by that fact that "she is seen by God." In the same Thru the Bible radio broadcast, he draws a modern-day comparison:

> "We've come as far short of seeing God as she does. It's difficult for a finite man to conceive of the infinite God, all of us come short of understanding and of knowing him. It's a theme that will engage us throughout the ages — coming to know God."

61

This would be Hagar's first experience with a deity who she experiences seeking her out. It would be her first understanding that God was paying attention to *her*. This is why she calls God, "El Roi" or "God who sees". This name for God is used thirty-four times in the Old Testament, and this passage in Genesis 16:13 is the very first time it is used. Again, the first mention principle is important.

This is a statement of truth that is upheld throughout the Bible: that God sees us (individually), that he knows us (individually), and that he is concerned for us (individually).

In Luke 15:4 we read Jesus words:

> *"Suppose one of you has a hundred sheep and loses one of them. Doesn't he leave the ninety-nine in the open country and go after the lost sheep until he finds it?"*

In that parable, Jesus is the Good Sheppard. In the story of Hagar, we see that parable reflected in the actions of the angel of the Lord (the pre-incarnate Christ): He has come into the wilderness to find Hagar, the one who fled from the flock. He pursues her.

It's important to understand this in relation to Hagar's state at that time. She was forced to conceive a child with her master, she suffered the abuse of Sarai, she fled the legal bond of her servitude, and she is taking away the child of her master that she carries. How horrible she must have felt, how lost she must have felt, how great was the loss of control over her person, her body, and her life. And yet, God pursues her. He doesn't pursue her to punish her, or to admonish her. It's clearly evident from the text of the passage that he deals with her, as Dr McGee said, "graciously." God is pursuing the one that needs him most.

This is an important lesson for the modern world. God pursues those who are farthest from him. Those who have done so much wrong, who have turned away from Him, who are running away from Him — these are the ones that God pursues the hardest: those who need him the most. The modern world can take solace from understanding that no matter what you have done, who you are, or what you are hiding from, God loves you and wants you to come to him, no matter what.

Hagar's Act of Faith

Hagar is told by the angel to return to her mistress and to submit herself under her hands. To gain an understanding of what Hagar must have gone through at this moment and in the hours to come, imagine a modern day pregnant woman finally fleeing a mentally, emotionally, and physically abusive relationship. The first person she meets and trusts looks her right in the eye and tells her to go back to the relationship.

The angel told Hagar to return to that despicable situation she had fled. The angel was telling her to submit herself to whatever punishment and work that was given to her. Taken in context, he was also telling her to honour her agreement to bear the child and to know her place, acting accordingly. The angel further promises that she will have a son and she will call him Ishmael. The angel also promises Hagar that she is going to have so many descendants, they cannot be counted. Hagar does return to her mistress and bears Abram a son when Abram is 86 years old (and he would still have many more sons).

> *"She gave this name to the Lord who spoke to her: "You are the God who sees me," for she said, "I have now seen the One who sees me." (Genesis 16:13)*

This part of the story is a bold demonstration of the faith that Hagar has spring forth in her for the God who sees her (El Roi). She understands that she has a place in His plan; she understands that He is with her and will be with her because she now understands that He *has* been with her.

John Gill's *Exposition of the Entire Bible* explains this much better than I can[37]:

> "... thou God seest me; she perceived by experience his eye was upon her wherever she was, and saw all she did; saw all her transgressions, her contempt of her mistress, and her flight from her; saw her when she was at the fountain, and reproved and recalled her, and sent her back; saw all the workings of her heart, her repentance and sorrow for her sins; looked and smiled upon her, and gave her exceeding great and precious promises: he looked upon her, both with his eye of omniscience and providence, and with his eye of love, and grace, and mercy; yea, she was sensible that he was not only the God that saw her, but saw all things; was God omniscient, and therefore gives him this name under a thorough

64

conviction and deep sense of his omniscience; and so Onkelos paraphrases the words, "thou art he, the God that sees all things;""

What faith! Coming from polytheistic Egypt, the monotheistic concept of one God would have been foreign to her from the start. However, when she was given to Sarai by Pharaoh, she became exposed to Abram's monotheistic belief. In the previously quoted Rabbinical commentary[31], Hagar was given as a slave (the word used in the commentary) after Pharaoh became aware of the power of Abram's God who was protecting Sarai. Hagar would undoubtedly have been aware of these things even if not witness to them. The experience she had when she fled would have changed awareness to experience.

In her time with Abram's family, Hagar would have been exposed to not only the worship of the one God, but also the power of God. She would have been witness to the events surrounding the battle with King Chedorlaomer at the Salt Lake. She would have been privy to the rescue of Lot. She would have been present when the Lord and two angels visited Abram. Hagar would have been distant witness to the destruction that the Lord rained down on Sodom and Gomorrah. But now, at the well of *Beer Lahai Roi* (Genesis 16:14), she was personally experiencing God's power and His love.

We see Hagar's faith emerging in this verse where she called out the name of the Lord. That means she called it out loud. The name she actually said was *"El Roi"*[38] ("God who sees"). Hagar was making an exclamation of surprise; with all that she had been through, all she had experienced, all she had given up, and all she had to deal with, she finally finds out that God is paying attention to *her*.

As with many of us, we may speak to God on a regular basis, but we don't actually acknowledge his attention to us until the chips are down and the piper is waiting to get paid. God is always paying attention to us, but we often miss the normal ways in which He pays attention to us. Our health, income, housing, food, familial bonds, clothes, the clean water in our taps, the gas in the tank in our car, our vocations, and so many more blessings come from God's attention to us. These are all blessings given to us by the Grace of our Lord. Without him, we would not have a life of blessings, we would be struggling for every tiny incremental move forward. Sadly, it is when we reach crucial points of conflict in our life that we are suddenly reminded of the One who loves us without hesitation. The One who suddenly becomes very obvious in our lives with the power and grace he brings to it. This is the kind of situation Hagar was in when suddenly, God sends one of His own angels to speak with her.

Undoubtedly, as with all of Abram's retinue, she would have been led to worship Abram's God. She would have taken on the mechanics of worship in her new surroundings. As an Egyptian Princess, she would have known that it was always politically correct to worship the local god where she was. In this case, the local god was the God of Abram. The only time an Egyptian would have direct interaction with one of their pantheon of deities would be when a high priest was in the performance of their duties. The eclectic pantheon of Egyptian gods did not interact with their worshipers (because they are false gods). Hagar not only finds herself in the desert, in the wilderness, anger, bitter, scared, and alone; she finds herself in the presence of God's personal messenger. Her acceptance and worship of the God of Abram suddenly became real in a very personal way. Abram's God was no longer merely the object of the mechanics of worship.

After she is told to return to her mistress, she returns without protest or complaint. We never actually hear another peep from her until she is expelled from the household. If you compare this to the story of Moses and the burning bush (Exodus 3 and Exodus 4:1-13), we see a very different response. I've actually found this story of Moses to be quite comical when you take a step back from how important it is. God has to do some pretty hard convincing to get Moses on board, while Moses is doing a whole lot of complaining. Not so with Hagar, she was told what to do, and she did it without any fuss. Hagar was immediately obedient to God's word, an obedience that was not born out of fear, but rather, was born out of faith (belief).

With this story, we again see a juxtaposition of responses when compared to the Israelites wandering the desert for forty years. In this part of the story of Hagar, Hagar wants to follow God's word because of her love (respect, appreciation) for him, not because of her fear of him. One of the themes of Deuteronomy is that the children of Israel wandered the desert for so long because it took that much time for them to learn to love the law, the covenant they re-established in Deuteronomy, rather than be a tribe following the covenant out of fear. This is another lesson we take from Hagar's story.

Follow the word and teachings of God out of your love for God, not out of fear.

The Israelites, the chosen ones, took forty years to get it together. Hagar did it in one day. The lesson to be taken from this is that God's love and caring are not only for the Israelites, the chosen ones. God's love is universal and is for all who will accept it from Him.

We find in Genesis 21:1-2 that God fulfilled his promise from Genesis 18:10, that Sarai would bear a son for Abram. Their son Isaac was born 1896 BCE (2108 AM)[16], when Abraham was 100 years old and Sarah was 90 years old. Sarah had already passed the time of life (menopause) that she could have children, but the Lord opened her womb again to fulfil his promise.

Sarai's Anger Towards Ishmael

Our story picks up in Genesis 21:8 when we learn that Isaac grew and was weaned, so Abraham had a great feast on the day he was weaned. We have no evidence that such a celebration is a common practice in Hebrew culture. Since the child arrived so late in life and was explicitly an act of God (the child was the promise of Spirit, whereas Ishmael is the Child of the Law), it's no doubt that there was much need to celebrate this milestone.

Additionally, the child having been weaned would mean he was past the usual maladies and disorders of an infant. This celebration would be a thanksgiving for passing this milestone and moving on to the next phase of childhood. How long did it take to wean him? There is nothing that tells us this for sure. We know that a child can be breastfed until any practical age. Ann Sinnott tells us that the World Health Organization recommends weaning for at least two years and beyond[39]. The 18th-century theologian John Gill in his *Exposition of the Entire Bible* relating to Genesis 22:1 tells us how varied the opinion of Jewish authors are when it comes to the question of how old Isaac was when he was weaned[40]. As we have used the works of Bishop Ussher for dating other events in this story, we find that Bishop Ussher placed this event when Isaac was five years old in 1891 BCE (2113 AM)[16].

> *"And the child grew, and was weaned: and Abraham made a great feast the same day that Isaac was weaned. And Sarah saw the son of Hagar the Egyptian, which she had born unto Abraham, mocking." (Genesis 21:8-9)*

If Isaac were weaned at age five, this would make Ishmael 14 or 15 years old. During the celebration, Sarah looks over and sees Hagar's son Ishmael mocking her own son, Isaac. While it doesn't take much effort to imagine what this mocking might have been, it really sets off Sarah! How dare he? This unrecognised son of her husband dared to mock her husband's legitimate and promised son? Their child, born of the promise of the Spirit, born of the promise of God, was the miracle child born to a woman well beyond the years of bearing children. The mockery would have been a horrible experience for Sarah.

Roughly fourteen years after the original drama, we see that Hagar's position has not improved. Apparently, the somewhat cordial relationship she originally had with Sarah did not return. Already having no love for Hagar because of their situation and Hagar's previous behaviour, this was gasoline on the fire, this was the final straw.

> *"Wherefore she said unto Abraham, Cast out this bondwoman and her son: for the son of this bondwoman shall not be heir with my son, even with Isaac. And the thing was very grievous in Abraham's sight because of his son. And God said unto Abraham, Let it not be grievous in thy sight because of the lad, and because of thy bondwoman; in all that Sarah hath said unto thee, hearken unto her voice; for in Isaac shall thy seed be called. And also of the son of the bondwoman will I make a nation, because he is thy seed."* (Genesis 21:10-13)

Sarah is so mad that she goes to her husband and begs Abraham to turn out Hagar and her son. Now that she has a child by her own womb, she does not want Ishmael, her great shining reminder of her lack of faith in God, to inherit anything from Abraham. She wants it all to go to Isaac. Under the tradition of this time, the firstborn son would inherit a double portion to all other sons (Deuteronomy 21:17). However, for this to happen, Ishmael would have had to have been legitimised, acknowledged, by Abraham.

Where the verse says Abraham finds the situation grievous, it doesn't really do justice to what Abraham faced. His wife of decades, the mother of his son, born of the promise of the Spirit, has asked him to turn out his first son and son's mother into the wilderness. Surely Abraham knows this is as close to a death sentence as he could get with them. Yet Ishmael is Abraham's firstborn son, born of his seed. The mother was given to him by his wife, but while Hagar should mean nothing to him, other than as the woman who bore Ishmael, Ishmael is still his son. Sarah is asking Abraham to turn out his first child, be he of the promise or of the flesh, she is still asking that his first son be cast into the wilderness like rubbish.

Imagine if you had a child before your marriage and your new spouse demanded that you cast the child into the world with a loaf of bread, a bottle of water, and were never to see them again. The only saving grace for either Abraham or Sarah in this situation is Abraham's faith. Hagar has her faith as well, and it will be tested, but Abraham turns to the Lord for guidance in what to do. He can't just reject it out of hand because Abraham knows that God has promised a nation will be born from his seed with Sarah (Genesis 17:15-16). Isaac is the child of Sarah, who was promised to him by God (Child of the Promise). Ishmael may not have been the promised son, but he was still Abraham's first born son (Child of the Law).

We find in Genesis 21:12 a very powerful and moving component of this story. God not only tells Abraham to relax, but He also expresses His love for Sarah, for Ishmael, and for Isaac. God wants Abraham to be supportive of Sarah as a loving husband should be. God has compassion for Sarah and Abraham in this situation, a situation ostensibly created entirely by Sarah's lack of faith. God also has compassion for Hagar and Ishmael. We hear God once again, as in Genesis 17:20, promise Abraham that Ishmael will be taken care of and will do well; that an entire nation will be made from his seed.

"Early the next morning Abraham took some food and a skin of water and gave them to Hagar. He set them on her shoulders and then sent her off with the boy. She went on her way and wandered in the Desert of Beersheba." (Genesis 21:14)

Because they are so easily put out of the household, we must assume that Ishmael had not been legitimised (acknowledged) by Abraham. Had he been legitimised, this banishment would never have been considered. Had he been legitimised by Abraham, Ishmael would have been entitled to the larger share of the inheritance of Abraham's estate, as his firstborn. However, since Abraham does not give an inheritance to Ishmael, we know he was not legitimised and can surmise that Hagar would have felt that her whole situation for the last fifteen years had been in vain.

The Expulsion of Hagar and Ishmael

Hagar's situation now was, once again, a situation of her nightmares come true. God had promised her before Ishmael's birth that Ishmael would be the father of a great nation. She most likely would have felt this would come from his lineage and eventual inheritance from Abraham. Within a few short years after Isaac's birth, she finds her son and herself being turned out of the camp and sent off to the wilderness. Adding to the disaster of this situation, Hagar had been with Abraham's household for twenty-five years! Most of her life had now been spent with them, and suddenly, with no warning, she is being turned away from all that she knows and is facing the wilderness of Beersheba (Beer Sheva), the Negev Desert, with her son. Only a loaf of bread and some water, with the vastness of Beersheba in front of her, what was she to do?

"And the water was spent in the bottle, and she cast the child under one of the shrubs. And she went, and sat her down over against him a good way off, as it were a bowshot: for she said, Let me not see the death of the child. And she sat over against him, and lift up her voice, and wept. And God heard the voice of the lad; and the angel of God called to Hagar out of heaven, and said unto her, What aileth thee, Hagar? fear not; for God hath heard the voice of the lad where he is. Arise, lift up the lad, and hold him in thine hand; for I will make him a great nation. And God opened her eyes, and she saw a well of water; and she went, and filled the bottle with water, and gave the lad drink." (Gen 21:15-19)

As they wandered in the Negev, things got worse. The water, life blood in the desert, was gone. All hope was gone. She didn't think this was the original plan of God. As far as she knew, Abraham and Sarah had changed the game on her. Tired, thirsty, and with waning hope, Hagar knows the end is going to come soon for them. Being without water in the Negev Desert would be an automatic death sentence for anyone else. Losing hope and being unable to bear what she knew was going to happen, she has her teenage son get under a shrub, for the shade. Being unable to bear watching the inevitable happen, she walks a couple hundred feet away and sits down to wait. Being a good ways off, she would not have heard the moans of suffering and thirst. Where verse 16 says *"she sat over against him"* means she had to harden her heart[41]. She could not watch what was going to happen; she could not watch her son die as he must in this situation.

Reaching one of those crucial pivot points in life, a point where we are stripped down to our barest and most humble self when the world seems surmounted against us, Hagar did what all of us do in that situation. She called out to God. Hagar lifted her voice and wept. This is where Hagar is reminded she is not walking alone, as none of us walks alone when we have God in our life. Hearing the child and by virtue of the connection of the story, hearing Hagar, God responds through his angel. The angel appears and asks why she has lost faith, thereby reminding her to have faith. The angel responds to her cry and tells her that God has heard the child's voice. This is the angel's way of telling her she worries for nothing, for God is with them always. The angel tells her to pick up the child and take him by the hand, which tells her that they both will survive and continue. The Lord then opens her eyes, and she sees a well before her. The water, given to Ishmael, heals him from dehydration and restores him to health.

Even though her faith has been challenged, God has not forsaken her. Instead, He is still paying very close attention to her, seeking her out once more, thus reinforcing the message that when we are at the most precarious points in our life, God is there for us, waiting only for us to call upon Him.

The phrase *"opens her eyes"* we find in a similar manner in more than one place (Numbers 22:31, Acts 26:18, Luke 24:31, Matthew 9:30, etc.) This doesn't mean the well wasn't there, it means that she couldn't see it. She could have been sand-blind from the desert, she could have had swollen eyes from being so long in the sun, she could simply have been so fearfully in tears she didn't see it. Of course, since this is an intervention by God, it's just as likely that the well really was not there before this, it merely came into existence when God created it for them. Regardless, they now had water; they now had life. Hagar sets her fears aside and once again allows herself to feel the love and devotion of God.

This is a very crucial lesson we learn from this story. It is a theme that if looked for, is found time and time again. To say that Hagar's life was less than ideal, if not downright difficult, would be an understatement. Yet through all of this, God is devoted to her, devoted to the big plan for her. Even though she goes through difficult times, He is still there watching over her just as He is still there, watching over you. When it comes down to crunch time and is absolutely needed, he responds as is necessary.

The Water of Life

I can't understate the importance of water in this story. Hagar is exiled with a small amount of water. When it runs out, her son is close to death and she soon will be too. Yet, when the angel of the Lord appears (the pre-incarnate Christ), he restores her son with water.

Jesus as the living water is a recurring theme in the New Testament, while God as the living water is a recurring theme in the Old Testament. With so many First Appearances in this story of Hagar, it cannot be lost on the reader that the pre-incarnate Christ (the angel of the Lord) is declaring His divinity, and tying the Old Testament to the New Testament with the concept of water-bringing life.

With the child almost dead, the angel of the Lord shows Hagar the well of water, the life-giving water, which restores the child. Keep in mind where this was taking place. Genesis 21:15 tells us they, *"wandered in the Desert of Beersheba."* The Old Testament Beersheba was the southernmost city of the land of the Bible. It was the last fertile land before the forbidding Negev Desert[42]. Since the passage says she wanted in the Desert of Beersheba, we know that she wandered into the Negev Desert:

> "The Negev in southern Israel can be oppressively hot, but you won't see the type of sand dunes associated with the Sahara or other deserts. Actually, the Negev is filled more with dirt, rocks and canyons, which are no less forbidding."[43]

Erik Lutz writes[44]:

> "Numerous Old Testament passages also use the vivid imagery of a dry, thirsty wilderness to portray our need as humans for the life-giving water of God's Spirit. The prophets often used water as a picture of salvation, …"

Author, blogger, and speaker Lois Tverberg explains the concept of living water in the Old Testament[45]:

> For the Israelites, the presence of rain in Israel was very much associated with blessing by God, and its absence with his disapproval. Almost every prophet decreed that drought would come as a punishment for their sins. But God's redemption was likened to him sending abundant rain, giving them living water to drink:

> *Then will the eyes of the blind be opened and the ears of the deaf unstopped. Then will the lame leap like a deer, and the mute tongue shout for joy. Water will gush forth in the wilderness and streams in the desert. The burning sand will become a pool, the thirsty ground bubbling springs. (Isaiah 35:5-7)*

> Because living water came directly from God, it was closely associated with God's Spirit in the world. When God promised to redeem his people, he promised to send his Spirit:

> *For I will pour out water on the thirsty land, and streams on the dry ground; I will pour out My Spirit on your offspring and My blessing on your descendants; and they will spring up among the grass like poplars by streams of water. (Isaiah 44:3 – 4)*

An important understanding of the "living water" that Jesus offers comes from the New Testament in John 4:4-14. Again, we find a woman at well whom Jesus is waiting for:

"4 Now he had to go through Samaria. 5 So he came to a town in Samaria called Sychar, near the plot of ground Jacob had given to his son Joseph. 6 Jacob's well was there, and Jesus, tired as he was from the journey, sat down by the well. It was about noon.

7 When a Samaritan woman came to draw water, Jesus said to her, "Will you give me a drink?" 8 (His disciples had gone into the town to buy food.)

9 The Samaritan woman said to him, "You are a Jew and I am a Samaritan woman. How can you ask me for a drink?" (For Jews do not associate with Samaritans.[a])

10 Jesus answered her, "If you knew the gift of God and who it is that asks you for a drink, you would have asked him and he would have given you living water."

11 "Sir," the woman said, "you have nothing to draw with and the well is deep. Where can you get this living water? 12 Are you greater than our father Jacob, who gave us the well and drank from it himself, as did also his sons and his livestock?"

13 Jesus answered, "Everyone who drinks this water will be thirsty again, 14 but whoever drinks the water I give them will never thirst. Indeed, the water I give them will become in them a spring of water welling up to eternal life.""

Commenting on this passage, Dr. Charles Stanley writes[46]:

"Like the Samaritan woman, we can at times be so intent on getting our immediate needs met that we fail to see God's hand reaching out to us in love, offering what will truly satisfy. Only Christ can fill our empty souls for eternity and provide for our essential emotional needs now.

This world is filled with wells that promise to provide love, acceptance, and self-worth but never fully satisfy. When your soul is empty and the well runs dry, look for Jesus. He has a divine appointment scheduled with you, and He will quench your thirst with His Spirit—if you let Him."

As well (pardon the pun) as being the living water of life, the imagery of water is about hope. As we read on in the chapter, we find that the woman has been married five times. Obviously, they had been difficult marriages or she would still have been with the first one. By the time she gets to the sixth husband, she isn't even married, she's just living with him. She is speaking from a place of immorality. She is lost, and without hope, just as Hagar is without hope; yet Jesus didn't criticize her.

In this story from John 4, the woman hangs a lantern on the fact that He, a Jew, is speaking with a Samaritan. Again, we see Jesus reaching beyond the Hebrew world, just as the pre-incarnate Christ did with Hagar, the Egyptian. Again, as we learned with the story of Hagar, the message is that no one is beyond God's redemption and love. Additionally, the message is strong and clear from both the story of the Samaritan woman at the well, and the story of Hagar, that no one is beyond hope.

To round off this discussion on water, the importance of the theme of water throughout the Bible is seen in the Book of Revelation:

"Then the angel showed me the river of the water of life, as clear as crystal, flowing from the throne of God and of the Lamb 2 down the middle of the great street of the city. On each side of the river stood the tree of life, bearing twelve crops of fruit, yielding its fruit every month. And the leaves of the tree are for the healing of the nations." *(Revelation 22:1-2)*

Bringing Hagar's Story to a Close

My study of the Bible so far has shown me that God likes to give tests. He likes to see how his children's faith is doing. The best way to test faith is to put a person in a situation where they only have faith to hold on to. What will they do? Will they turn to the world and the understanding of men or will they turn to Him? The Lord has done this to me as He has done to countless people. An important lesson we need to take from the story of Hagar is about maintaining faith in God, even when it seems God has forgotten you. He hasn't forgotten you, He is there, He moves in his own time and in His own way. It is not for us to understand God's mind or intentions (1 Corinthians 2:11), rather, it is for us to simply have and maintain our faith always.

"20 God was with the boy as he grew up. He lived in the desert and became an archer. 21 While he was living in the Desert of Paran, his mother got a wife for him from Egypt." *(Gen 21:20-21)*

So, our story ends. Hagar and Ishmael are saved. They move on to dwell in the wilderness of Paran. We know that Ishmael is the father of twelve tribes (twelve sons) and that his seed is multiplied beyond numbering. Modern day Islam holds that Ishmael is the father of the Arab nation, the forefather of the Prophet Muhammed. Ishmael lives to an age of 137 years (Genesis 25:17), passing away in 1773 BCE (2231 AM)[16].

The rest of Hagar's life is not accounted for in the Bible unless you believe the Rabbinical commentary that claims Hagar was Abraham's second wife, Keturah[47]. From what we have seen of Hagar's character and what we know of the character and skills of her son Ishmael, I have no doubt she lived a long life and did indeed watch her son become a nation. She would have persevered through her strength, courage, and faith.

Chapter 7
Summary

In the story of Hagar, we can take away several lessons. These apply to both men and women, regardless of birth, position, or station.

Surrender: Faith, Courage, and Strength

I believe that the biggest lesson we learn from Hagar's story is about surrender. Earlier in this book, I spoke about the loss of control. It's important to understand that feeling as you read Hagar's story to understand what she may have been feeling. However, understanding the loss of control is not the lesson. The lesson comes from learning how to *surrender* control.

After Hagar had conceived, it says that Hagar began to despise her mistress. I think this would be perfectly understandable. Not only had Hagar lost the control over her life in that she was forced to become a servant, she additionally had now lost control over her own body as she was being forced to use it for another's pleasure and another's gain. Add to this very personal loss of control to the daily life that was inherent to her role, she must have, after the conception, quickly reached quite a state of frustration, if not outright anger. Reacting to this compounding loss of control, she finally can't take it anymore. Perhaps it would be more precise to say she didn't feel she could take it anymore by herself.

On her own, Hagar flees to the wilderness, but very quickly finds that she is not alone. An angel of the Lord appears to her. I think the quick appearance of the angel is a very good allegory for God's ever-presence in our lives. Hagar's flight from Abram's family was her own cry for help, and God responded to her. Her cry for help did not go unnoticed. Unfortunately, it wasn't quite the response she would have wanted. How many times has that happened to you?

Instead of whisking her off to safety, plentiful food and water, as well as a comfortable life, God (through His angel) tells her to go back to Sarai and "submit" to her. This had to be the absolute last thing the poor woman wanted to hear. Go back willingly to what she had just come from? The angel was asking her to surrender her will to that of the Lord, to do as the Lord asked out of trust. This also meant that when she returned, she would have to continue to surrender her control to Sarai and Abram. The angel did promise her that in the end, her son would survive and that she would have many descendants (a good thing in those days). Still, the prospect of having to return to Sarai's horrible treatment would have been daunting.

Hagar did choose to return and submit to Sarai, just as the angel of the Lord had told her. Hagar chose to surrender to the will of God, to surrender to what He wanted her to do. She did have a choice. She didn't have to go back. She could have got up and kept on walking into the desert, but she didn't. Having been exposed for ten years to the monotheism of her master's household, she said, *"I have now seen the One who sees me"*. She acknowledged God and with that statement, submitted herself or more rightly, surrendered herself to His will.

In our lives, how many times have we been faced with difficult times or difficult situations and called on God for help, only to find Him silent or unresponsive or responding in a way we didn't want? If we are faithful, practice brotherly love, follow Jesus' example on how to live our lives, then why are we not getting the immediate treatment we think we deserve? God has given mankind free will. We are free to do and think and believe as we please. While a discussion on free will would take up several books, for this discussion we can form an understanding from Proverbs 16:9, *"The heart of man plans his way, but the Lord establishes his steps."*

I remember a time in my life that was filled with turmoil, lack of direction, indecision, and everything was simply horrible. Nothing was working, and nothing was going my way. I remember sitting on the couch one day and saying whatever you have to do, my life is crap, my way doesn't work. Please change my life for the better, whatever you have to do, I surrender.

Within a few short months, I had lost my job, lost my house, and lost my wife. It really didn't seem at that point that things had gotten better. Looking back at that time, from over ten years in the future, I can say that everything I went through, I had to go through to get where I am today; and where I am today is much, much better. Sometimes the slings and arrows of outrageous fortune (Shakespeare) are merely part of God clearing away the debris to build something new.

We decide who we are, what our character is, what values we have, what we want to achieve in life, what our goals are, how we treat people, how we worship, how we interact with those around us. We plan the way. The verse from Proverbs tells us that while it is our freedom to do this, God is not absent from our plan. God will be marking out the steps that we take. Not every individual minute step, I mean the milestones, the waypoints, the significant (and some not-so-significant) events. We still have the option of not following the way that God has set out for us. Sometimes this is because the way that God has charted for us just seems too hard to handle or too much to face. Speaking from personal experience, sometimes the way that God has charted for us takes us deeper into trouble or deeper into scary places. However, it's not fighting these changes or situations that will get us through them; it is surrendering to God's will that will get us through them. If you resist going down a difficult path, do you think that the next path will be easier? Or the next? Or the next one? Sometimes the only way to get past the difficulty is to go directly through the middle of the difficulty. This doesn't mean you don't protect yourself, this doesn't mean you don't plan contingencies for yourself; this doesn't mean you don't defend yourself; this doesn't mean you don't pray to God for help. It does mean that when you are faced with difficulty and have no way around that difficulty, perhaps you just need to surrender yourself to God's will and let Him guide your actions. Place the difficulty in his hands and trust in God to get you where He wants you to be.

"Do not be anxious about anything, but in every situation, by prayer and petition, with thanksgiving, present your requests to God." (Philippians 4:6)

As much as it can frustrate or infuriate us, there are times that we must be subject to the control of another person, entity, or law. There are simply some situations where we must surrender control and ride the currents of the moment. Sometimes we simply have to resign our self-appointed position "as general manager of the universe" (paraphrasing Larry Eisenberg).

God's Omnipresence

The lesson of surrender is directly related to the lesson that we don't know better than God. God is omniscient, He sees and knows all. And as such, we cannot know what it is that He knows, unless He shares it with us.

"We do, however, speak a message of wisdom among the mature, but not the wisdom of this age or of the rulers of this age, who are coming to nothing. No, we declare God's wisdom, a mystery that has been hidden and that God destined for our glory before time began. None of the rulers of this age understood it, for if they had, they would not have crucified the Lord of glory. However, as it is written:

"What no eye has seen, what no ear has heard, and what no human mind has conceived" — the things God has prepared for those who love him —

these are the things God has revealed to us by his Spirit.

The Spirit searches all things, even the deep things of God. For who knows a person's thoughts except their own spirit within them? In the same way no one knows the thoughts of God except the Spirit of God." (1 Corinthians 2:6-11)

"For as the heavens are higher than the earth, so are my ways higher than your ways and my thoughts than your thoughts." (Isaiah 55:9)

This is an important lesson in the story of Hagar, a lesson that reminds us not only to surrender to God, but just as importantly to trust in God. We need to trust that God knows far more and far better than we do. This is the story of Sarai's doubt. God promised Abram that he would have a child of his own flesh and blood (Genesis 12:2, 12:7, 13:15-16, 15:4-5, 15:18). After the birth of Ishmael, God appears to Abraham and Sarah in human form, and still, she (Sarah) doesn't believe him (Genesis 18:1-15). Sure enough, though, at the time that God had appointed, Sarah became pregnant and delivered a healthy bouncing baby Isaac (Genesis 21:1-3).

Sarah was well past childbearing age (Genesis 18:11) or in biblical terms, her womb was closed. However, God promised that she would have a child. Is nothing impossible for God? Of course not! At the age of ninety (Genesis 17:17, Genesis 21:2) Sarah gave birth to Isaac. She gave birth to the child that was conceived through divine intervention, through the promise of the Spirit. Ishmael was conceived through the arrangements of people, not through the intervention of spirit. This is why Isaac is referred to as the Child of the Promise, and Ishmael is referred to as the Child of the Flesh or the Child of the Law

"It is not as though God's word had failed. For not all who are descended from Israel are Israel. Nor because they are his descendants are they all Abraham's children. On the contrary, "It is through Isaac that your offspring will be reckoned." In other words, it is not the children by physical descent who are God's children, but it is the children of the promise who are regarded as Abraham's offspring. For this was how the promise was stated: "At the appointed time I will return, and Sarah will have a son."" (Romans 9:6-9)

"His son by the slave woman was born according to the flesh, but his son by the free woman was born as the result of a divine promise." (Galatians 4:23)

Galatians 4:21-31 deals exclusively with the New Testament view of Hagar and Sarah and is recommended for you to read.

The Child of the Flesh, Ishmael, arrived from Sarah's impatience and her lack of trust in God's promise. God had the long view; He had a plan, and that plan unfolded at His timing and pace. Sarah didn't trust Him, and she jumped the gun. Had she left well enough alone, she would have had her son and would not have had the drama with Hagar. How much drama in your life could have been averted if you had just surrendered to God's will and not tried to force things according to your own plan?

"Trust in the LORD with all your heart and lean not on your own understanding; in all your ways submit to him, and he will make your paths straight" (Proverbs 3:5-6)

As I stated, this was Hagar's first experience with a deity seeking her out. In fact, it's the first time God is called "El Roi", the one who sees me. This is a vital lesson to take from the story. God is not just a heaven-hovering distant deity, He is concerned for each of us, and He sees each one of us.

God's Forgiveness

We find in Genesis 21:12 a very powerful and moving component of this story. God not only tells Abraham to relax, but He also expresses His love for Sarah, for Ishmael, and for Isaac. God wants Abraham to be supportive of Sarah as a loving husband should be. God has compassion for Sarah and Abraham in this situation, a situation ostensibly created entirely by Sarah's lack of faith. God also has compassion for Hagar and Ishmael. We hear God once again, as in Genesis 17:20, promise Abraham that Ishmael will be taken care of and will do well; that an entire nation will be made from his seed.

"Early the next morning Abraham took some food and a skin of water and gave them to Hagar. He set them on her shoulders and then sent her off with the boy. She went on her way and wandered in the Desert of Beersheba." (Genesis 21:14)

Because they are so easily put out of the household, we must assume that Ishmael had not been legitimised (acknowledged) by Abraham. Had he been legitimised, this banishment would never have been considered. Had he been legitimised by Abraham, Ishmael would have been entitled to the larger share of the inheritance of Abraham's estate, as his firstborn. However, since Abraham does not give an inheritance to Ishmael, we know he was not legitimised and can surmise that Hagar would have felt that her whole situation for the last fifteen years had been in vain.

No One is Lost

I was once in a state of mind that I thought I had strayed too far from God, and done things too horrible for him to still want me. At times when I wanted to turn to Him, I was afraid to. No, actually, I was ashamed to. I had grown up in a Christian household and had a strong faith as a child. At some point in my adult life, I turned my back on God. When I realised I was wrong for doing that, I was suffering from depression which fueled the shame that kept me from inviting him back into my life.

Finally, things got so bad that a friend said, "Jim, it's time to let go, and let God." I gave it a shot and what do you know? He was right there waiting for me. From that moment, my life changed. It didn't change in that things became less complicated, but it changed in that it got easier walking through those things with God.

When Hagar flees to the desert while pregnant, God is there for her. He hears her cries and responds to them. Hagar was not a Hebrew, she was not a man (who were the principal characters to that point), she was not a believer. In fact, she came from a pagan world and a pagan home. There she was, breaking the law by fleeing Abram's household, and kidnapping his unborn child. Did God punish her? Accost her? Have her arrested? No. Instead, God loved her. God treated her well and helped her. God reached out to her, and she listened.

No matter who you are, no matter what you have done, God is not beyond your reach. Approach him with a contrite and repentant heart, truly desire His presence in your life, and ask Him to take control. He is there, He is waiting — you only have to ask.

Trusting God

Surrender and trust come to us more easily by knowing that God is ever present in our lives. God loves us and never abandons us. The idea of God abandoning us would be incomprehensible to Him. If we look at the big picture of the story of Hagar, from the time Abram enters Egypt until the angel reveals the water well when Hagar and Ishmael are sent away, there is a master plan unfolding. There is a larger story that has many parts, and someone needs to be directing those parts and keeping them on track. This is God at work. When Hagar first flees Sarai during Hagar's pregnancy, we see God stepping to get things back on track. She wasn't alone, He was with her, and He was watching her. He stepped in when He needed to, so that she could remain on track for what was to come later. If we extrapolate forward using the quoted midrash and hadith, we see that she eventually did achieve a much better life as a free woman. However, none of that would have been achieved were it not for the birth of Ishmael. There was a bigger picture.

As this microcosm of Hagar's life is portrayed, so too, the macrocosm of our own lives has a plan. There are waypoints, milestones, and certain objectives that God wants us to reach. There is an overall plan, and God is at the helm, waiting for us to surrender control to Him. We make plans and decisions as we go through life (free will) and try not to go wildly off course from what God has in store for us. If we do, we may suddenly find ourselves encountering a correction of our course of actions or perhaps a gentle, or not-so-gentle, nudging to the correct decisions.

Blogger, public speaker, and inspirational speaker Rachel Wojnarowski has this to say on the matter of God's presence in our daily lives[48]:

"When I can't understand God's plan, there is a question I find myself asking:

Where is God in all this?

The more I've been reflecting on this question recently, the more I've realized that the problem is not where God is.

Because God is everywhere.

The problem is that I'm asking the wrong question. You see, the question I should be asking is:

Why can't I see God in this?"

Because His fingerprints are all over His handiwork. Even when bad things happen to good people, He molds and reshapes until you can't even recognize the bad anymore. It's a plan called "redemption."

So I've stopped asking God where He is. I mean, it's pretty obvious that He's been here since before the beginning of time and He's not going anywhere. The Alpha and Omega.

I've started asking Him to reveal Himself to me.

Lord, help me see Your work in this situation.

(Reprinted with permission)

God was also there and ever present for Abraham and Sarah, not only for Hagar. Even when Sarah doubted God and worked against His plan, He was still there to keep his promises to the couple. When Hagar and Ishmael were exiled, God was there for both of them as well, saving them from death and ensuring their bright future. Even when you may feel that God is ignoring you, He isn't. He is there, and He is there for you, even if you don't have the ability to see it at the time. Surrender to His love and His will — and be anxious for nothing (Philippians 4:6).

"I will fear no evil, for you are with me" (Psalm 23:4).

When Hagar was exiled with Ishmael, and when she reached a point she was sure her son would die, she, *"lifted her voice and wept."* And guess what? God heard her and responded. Hagar reached a point where she approached God with surrender to His will. Was it hopelessness, or was it a supreme statement of faith? Regardless, God allowed her to demonstrate her faith, and then He responded to her. As I said previously in the text of this book, even though her faith had been challenged, God has not forsaken her. Instead, He was still paying very close attention to her, seeking her out once more, thus reinforcing the message that when we are at the most precarious points in our life, God is there for us, waiting only for us to call upon Him and trust in Him.

The Christophany

There are some medieval commentators who believe that the Lord God's appearance in the Garden of Eden (Genesis 3:8) was a Christophany. However, the text very clearly states it is the Lord God. The original Hebrew text uses both the term *Elohim* (H430) which means the supreme God, and the term *Yahweh* (H3068) which means the self-Existent or Eternal, Jehovah, the Jewish national name for God[37].

There are some Christians who also consider Melchizedek (Genesis 14:18-20) to be a Christophany, although a source I once read claimed it was a Theophany.

Regardless, the angel of the Lord in Genesis 16 is the first Christophany agreed upon by all sources that I've researched. In Genesis 16:7, 9, and 11 we read "the" angel of the Lord and in Genesis 21:17 we read "the" angel of God", not "an" angel. Additionally, Genesis 21:17-19 seems very fluid in the wording in that it seamlessly changes from the angel of God to God. In verse 17 the text says, *"God has heard the boy crying ..."* and in verse 18 the angel says, *"... for*

I will make him into a great nation." This promise of a great nation is the fulfilment of the promise to Abram in Genesis 15. Since it is God's promise, it is God that is fulfilling it. This tells us quite clearly that since the text starts with the angel of God, this is the pre-incarnate Christ because only He, the second aspect of the Trinity, could make that promise aside from God Himself.

In the book, *Jesus Christ, our Lord*, Dr. John Walvoord states[49]:

> "The combined testimony of these passages portrays the Son of God as exceedingly active in the Old testament, dealing with sin, providing for those in need, guiding in the path of the will of God, protecting His people form their enemies and, in general, executing the providence of God. The references make plain that this ministry is not occasional or exceptional bur rather the common and continual ministry of God to His people. The revelation of the person of the Son of God thus afforded is in complete harmony with the New Testament revelation. The testimony of Scripture has been so complete on this point that in general scholars who accept the inspiration and infallibility of Scripture are agreed that the Angel of Jehovah is the Christ of the Old Testament. Not only Christian theologians but Jewish scholars as well have come to the conclusion that the Angel of Jehovah is more than an angel. It is once a revelation of the person and preincarnate work of Christ and an evidence for His preexistence and deity."

In *Coffman's Commentaries on the Bible*, "one of the finest modern conservative commentary sets written"[50], we read this about Genesis 16:9-11:

> "Thou shalt bear a son, and thou shalt call his name Ishmael ..." This recalls the prophecy of Gabriel to Mary. Only God can name in advance the sex of a child before it is conceived and bestow the name in the manner noted here."

So, what is the importance of this, beyond what I said earlier?

The pre-incarnate Christ treats Hagar with love and gentleness, while still demanding her act of faith. This is a foreshadowing of the Christ of the New Testament: the manner in which he treats others, and his Great Commission. Since we are seeing the second person of the Trinity in the Old Testament, this prepares us for the introduction of the Trinity as presented in the gospels and the Book of Acts.

The Christophanies are also important for our understanding of God in more than one form. He is God, and He is also Christ. The two are the same, but they are different. It enhances our view of the Divine nature as being beyond us, being unknowable, being Godly.

Finally, the appearance of the angel of the Lord demonstrates Christ's intercessory nature. In the New Testament, Christ's intercession as the Lamb of God was his intercession to save mankind through his sacrifice. In the Christophanies of the Old Testament, particularly with this first appearance, the pre-incarnate Christ is interceding in what Hagar may have suffered without him. This example reinforces the New Testament example that Christ sets, where we, as Christians, sometimes need to step up and speak out or act on behalf of others, for their betterment.

God Declares Himself

While I was discussing this book with my pastor, it was this phrase that he used to sum up what I was saying about God making his presence known, "God declares Himself". There are many ways that God declares (reveals) Himself in the Bible. It is through the Bible that we get to know God. In fact, it is the only way we get to know God apart from our own personal experience with Him. The Bible is the only source of revelation for God.

There are instances in the Bible of direct revelation or direct declaration where God states it unequivocally: I AM GOD.

Exodus 3:14 God reveals His name to Moses, *"I AM WHO I AM"*.

In response to his questioning, God tells of His limitless authority and wisdom in Job chapters 38 through 41.

Further, in Isaiah, we read:

> *"I am the LORD, the Maker of all things, who stretches out the heavens, who spreads out the earth by myself" (Isaiah 44:24)*

> *"I am the LORD, and there is no other; apart from me there is no God. I will strengthen you, though you have not acknowledged me," (Isaiah 45:5)*

"And there is no God apart from me, a righteous God and a Savior; there is none but me." (Isaiah 45:21)

"I am God, and there is no other; I am God, and there is none like me. I make known the end from the beginning, from ancient times, what is still to come. I say, 'My purpose will stand, and I will do all that I please.'" (Isaiah 46:9-10)

Throughout Exodus and Leviticus, there are many, many instances of God declaring Himself.

There are also examples where God makes Himself known through His works and His power, where He is revealed by example.

In Genesis 12:17, *"But the Lord inflicted serious diseases on Pharaoh and his household because of Abram's wife Sarai."* The Pharaoh knew this was coming from Abraham's God; therefore, God's power was demonstrated or revealed.

In Exodus 7 the Lord declares that He is doing something specifically so that the Egyptians will know His power and His omniscience (the ten plagues). He is also doing this, so they will know He is "THE" Lord, the one God.

"Then the LORD said to Moses, "See, I have made you like God to Pharaoh, and your brother Aaron will be your prophet. You are to say everything I command you, and your brother Aaron is to tell Pharaoh to let the Israelites go out of his country. But I will harden Pharaoh's heart, and though I multiply my signs and wonders in Egypt, he will not listen to you. Then I will lay my

hand on Egypt and with mighty acts of judgment I will bring out my divisions, my people the Israelites. And the Egyptians will know that I am the LORD when I stretch out my hand against Egypt and bring the Israelites out of it." (Exodus 7:1-5)

In the story of Hagar, we get a combination of direct revelation (God promises Abraham children at his old age), and we get revelation through the example of his power (opening Sarah's womb). We get direct revelation through the angel of the Lord's first encounter with Hagar and the example of His power through the second encounter (the water well).

In the middle of the story of Hagar, God sends two angels to Sodom and Gomorrah, and He is declared through the example of His power of destruction. In Exodus, a pillar of fire and pillar of smoke leads the Israelites from Egypt to the Red Sea. Also in Exodus, the Red Sea parts so the Israelites can flee from Pharaoh's army. There are many, many examples of God's direct power and intervention that through the example, declares God or as stated, reveals God.

Another kind of revelation of God is through nature and the world around us as the simplest forms of revelation. The act of Creation would be the first way that God reveals himself. Who created the heavens and the earth? God did! (Gen 1:1) This would also be an ongoing revelation/declaration through the ages and time, still as ever valid today as it was four thousand years ago. Just look at the world around you. Look at the intricacy and complexity. Merely chance chemical combinations? In Romans 1:20 we read:

"For since the creation of the world God's invisible qualities—his eternal power and divine nature—have been clearly seen, being understood from what has been made, so that people are without excuse."

King David tells us in Psalm 8:3-4 that the heavens, moon, and stars are a declaration of God as well:

"When I consider your heavens, the work of your fingers, the moon and the stars, which you have set in place, what is mankind that you are mindful of them, human beings that you care for them?"

Conclusion

The story of Hagar has several declarations by God. It is a powerful and revealing story that gives us much, much more than just the words, as I hope you will have seen. The faith that Hagar demonstrates in surrendering to God's will is an example we all need to be cognizant of. How incredibly strong her faith had to have been.

Mark Twain said, "Faith is something you know ain't true". Benjamin Franklin said, "The way to see by faith is to shut the eye of reason". How often have you heard derogatory statements like this? I've been accused of being foolish, being weak minded, and being uneducated (stupid) for my belief in God, Jesus, and the Bible. Being a faithful Christian takes strength.

It takes strength to stay the course and to trust in God. It takes courage to take the hard walks that God sometimes requires of us. It takes faithful perseverance to face the scrutiny and outright mockery of unbelievers.

Have you ever noticed how as soon as the topic of your faith comes up, you seem to be held to a higher standard than others? Hagar lived under Sarah and Abraham for twenty-five years. She was forced to conceive a child with another woman's husband, and when she tried to flee the horrible treatment resulting from what she was forced to do, God asked her to go back, and she did. That is not weakness. That is courage. That is strength. That is faith.

Doing what God wants is *not* always going to be easy for us, but it is always going to be right for us to do so. Keeping our faith in God's promises to us is vital. Otherwise, we just complicate matters. The courage and strength that Hagar displayed came from the surrender of her will to God's. It is not weakness to place our lives in the hands of God or to surrender our will to Him. Doing so requires great strength, a great deal of courage, and perhaps most of all, a great deal of faith. No one ever said being a faithful servant of God would be easy, but would you really want to have your life without Him in it? Unfortunately, that is only a question that can be answered by someone who has given their life over to God and experienced His love first hand.

Just as God loved Abraham, Sarah, Hagar, Ishmael and Isaac, so, too, that very self-same God loves you. Be strong, show courage, and have the faith of a poor maidservant alone in the desert.

Deus Caritas Est

Excerpts from the Book of Genesis

The following excerpts from the Book of Genesis (chapters 12, 16, 17 & 21) tell the story of Hagar from the New International Version (NIV). I have included these verses on the off chance that you do not have the blessing of a copy of the Holy Bible in your possession. If that is the case and you cannot obtain a copy of one (for one reason or another), here are options for you:

- You can read the Bible online at biblegateway.com. It includes numerous versions of the text.
- You can find the Bible as an app for your tablet or phone at youversion.com.
- An excellent study tool is blueletterbible.org which contains many versions of the text, as well as a powerful suite of study tools, all free.
- Do you attend church? Tell your pastor you need a bible. He will get you one.

Genesis 12

The Call of Abram

(1)The Lord had said to Abram, "Go from your country, your people and your father's household to the land I will show you.

(2)"I will make you into a great nation,

and I will bless you;

I will make your name great,

and you will be a blessing.

(3)I will bless those who bless you,

and whoever curses you I will curse;

and all peoples on earth

will be blessed through you."

(4)So Abram went, as the Lord had told him; and Lot went with him. Abram was seventy-five years old when he set out from Harran. (5)He took his wife Sarai, his nephew Lot, all the possessions they had accumulated and the people they had acquired in Harran, and they set out for the land of Canaan, and they arrived there. (6)Abram traveled through the land as far as the site of the great tree of Moreh at Shechem. At that time the Canaanites were in the land. (7)The Lord appeared to Abram and said, "To your offspring I will give this land." So he built an altar there to the Lord, who had appeared to him. (8)From there he went on toward the hills east of Bethel and pitched his tent, with Bethel on the west and Ai on the east. There he built an altar to the Lord and called on the name of the Lord. (9)Then Abram set out and continued toward the Negev.

Abram in Egypt

(10)Now there was a famine in the land, and Abram went down to Egypt to live there for a while because the famine was severe. (11)As he was about to enter Egypt, he said to his wife Sarai, "I know what a beautiful woman you are. (12)When the Egyptians see you, they will say, 'This is his wife.' Then they will kill me but will let you live. (13)Say you are my sister, so that I will be treated well for your sake and my life will be spared because of you." (14)When Abram came to Egypt, the Egyptians saw that Sarai was a very beautiful woman. (15)And when Pharaoh's officials saw her, they praised her to Pharaoh, and she was taken into his palace. (16)He treated Abram well for her sake, and Abram acquired sheep and cattle, male and female donkeys, male and female servants, and camels. (17)But the Lord inflicted serious diseases on Pharaoh and his household because of Abram's wife Sarai. (18)So Pharaoh summoned Abram. "What have you done to me?" he said. "Why didn't you tell me she was your wife? (19)Why did you say, 'She is my sister,' so that I took her to be my wife? Now then, here is your wife. Take her and go!" (20)Then Pharaoh gave orders about Abram to his men, and they sent him on his way, with his wife and everything he had.

Genesis 16

Hagar and Ishmael

(1)Now Sarai, Abram's wife, had borne him no children. But she had an Egyptian slave named Hagar; (2)so she said to Abram, "The Lord has kept me from having children. Go, sleep with my slave; perhaps I can build a family through her." Abram agreed to what Sarai said. (3)So after Abram had been living in Canaan ten years, Sarai his wife took her

Egyptian slave Hagar and gave her to her husband to be his wife. (4)He slept with Hagar, and she conceived. When she knew she was pregnant, she began to despise her mistress. (5)Then Sarai said to Abram, "You are responsible for the wrong I am suffering. I put my slave in your arms, and now that she knows she is pregnant, she despises me. May the Lord judge between you and me." (6)"Your slave is in your hands," Abram said. "Do with her whatever you think best." Then Sarai mistreated Hagar; so she fled from her. (7)The angel of the Lord found Hagar near a spring in the desert; it was the spring that is beside the road to Shur. (8)And he said, "Hagar, slave of Sarai, where have you come from, and where are you going?" "I'm running away from my mistress Sarai," she answered. (9)Then the angel of the Lord told her, "Go back to your mistress and submit to her." (10)The angel added, "I will increase your descendants so much that they will be too numerous to count." (11)The angel of the Lord also said to her:

"You are now pregnant

and you will give birth to a son.

You shall name him Ishmael,

for the Lord has heard of your misery.

(12)He will be a wild donkey of a man;

his hand will be against everyone

and everyone's hand against him,

and he will live in hostility

toward all his brothers."

(13)She gave this name to the Lord who spoke to her: "You are the God who sees me," for she said, "I have now seen the One who sees me." (14)That is why the well was called Beer Lahai Roi ; it is still there, between Kadesh and Bered. (15)So Hagar bore Abram a son, and Abram gave the name Ishmael to the son she had borne. (16)Abram was eighty-six years old when Hagar bore him Ishmael.

Genesis 17

The Covenant of Circumcision

(1)When Abram was ninety-nine years old, the Lord appeared to him and said, "I am God Almighty ; walk before me faithfully and be blameless. (2)Then I will make my covenant between me and you and will greatly increase your numbers." (3)Abram fell facedown, and God said to him, (4)"As for me, this is my covenant with you: You will be the father of many nations. (5)No longer will you be called Abram ; your name will be Abraham, for I have made you a father of many nations. (6)I will make you very fruitful; I will make nations of you, and kings will come from you. (7)I will establish my covenant as an everlasting covenant between me and you and your descendants after you for the generations to come, to be your God and the God of your descendants after you. (8)The whole land of Canaan, where you now reside as a foreigner, I will give as an everlasting possession to you and your descendants after you; and I will be their God." (9)Then God said to Abraham, "As for you, you must keep my covenant, you and your descendants after you for the generations to come. (10)This is my covenant with you and your descendants after you, the covenant you are to keep: Every male among you shall be circumcised. (11)You are to undergo circumcision, and it will be the sign of the covenant between me and you. (12)For the generations to come every male among you who is eight days old must be circumcised, including those born in your household or bought with money from a foreigner—those who are not your offspring. (13)Whether born in your household or bought with your money, they must be circumcised. My covenant in your flesh is to be an everlasting covenant. (14)Any uncircumcised male, who has not been circumcised in the flesh, will be cut off from his people; he has broken my covenant." (15)God also said to Abraham, "As for Sarai your wife, you are no longer to call her Sarai; her name will be Sarah. (16)I will bless her and will surely give you a son by her. I will bless her so that she will be the mother of nations; kings of peoples will come from her." (17)Abraham fell facedown; he laughed and said to himself, "Will a son be born to a man a hundred years old? Will Sarah bear a child at the age of ninety?" (18)And Abraham said to God, "If only Ishmael might live under your blessing!" (19)Then God said, "Yes, but your wife Sarah will bear you a son, and you will call him Isaac. I will establish my covenant with him as an everlasting covenant for his descendants after him. (20)And as for Ishmael, I have heard you: I will surely bless him; I will make him fruitful and will greatly increase his numbers. He will be the father of twelve rulers, and I will make him into a great nation. (21)But my covenant I will establish with Isaac, whom Sarah will bear to you by this time next year." (22)When he had finished speaking with Abraham, God went up from him. (23)On that very day Abraham took his son Ishmael and all those born in his household or bought with his money, every male in his household, and circumcised them, as God told him. (24)Abraham was ninety-nine years old when he was circumcised, (25)and his son Ishmael was thirteen; (26)Abraham and his son Ishmael were both circumcised on that very day. (27)And every male in Abraham's household, including those born in his household or bought from a foreigner, was circumcised with him.

Genesis 21

The Birth of Isaac

(1)Now the Lord was gracious to Sarah as he had said, and the Lord did for Sarah what he had promised. (2)Sarah became pregnant and bore a son to Abraham in his old age, at the very time God had promised him. (3)Abraham gave the name Isaac to the son Sarah bore him. (4)When his son Isaac was eight days old, Abraham circumcised him, as God commanded him. (5)Abraham was a hundred years old when his son Isaac was born to him. (6)Sarah said, "God has brought me laughter, and everyone who hears about this will laugh with me." (7)And she added, "Who would have said to Abraham that Sarah would nurse children? Yet I have borne him a son in his old age."

Hagar and Ishmael Sent Away

(8)The child grew and was weaned, and on the day Isaac was weaned Abraham held a great feast. (9)But Sarah saw that the son whom Hagar the Egyptian had borne to Abraham was mocking, (10)and she said to Abraham, "Get rid of that slave woman and her son, for that woman's son will never share in the inheritance with my son Isaac." (11)The matter distressed Abraham greatly because it concerned his son. (12)But God said to him, "Do not be so distressed about the boy and your slave woman. Listen to whatever Sarah tells you, because it is through Isaac that your offspring will be reckoned. (13)I will make the son of the slave into a nation also, because he is your offspring." (14)Early the next morning Abraham took some food and a skin of water and gave them to Hagar. He set them on her shoulders and then sent her off with the boy. She went on her way and wandered in the Desert of Beersheba. (15)When the water in the skin was gone, she put the boy under one of the bushes. (16)Then she went off and sat down about a bowshot away, for she thought, "I cannot watch the boy die." And as she sat there, she began to sob. (17)God heard the boy crying, and the angel of God called to Hagar from heaven and said to her, "What is the matter, Hagar? Do not be afraid; God has heard the boy crying as he lies there. (18)Lift the boy up and take him by the hand, for I will make him into a great nation." (19)Then God opened her eyes and she saw a well of water. So she went and filled the skin with water and gave the boy a drink. (20)God was with the boy as he grew up. He lived in the desert and became an archer. (21)While he was living in the Desert of Paran, his mother got a wife for him from Egypt.

The Treaty at Beersheba

(22)At that time Abimelek and Phicol the commander of his forces said to Abraham, "God is with you in everything you do. (23)Now swear to me here before God that you will not deal falsely with me or my children or my descendants. Show to me and the country where you now reside as a foreigner the same kindness I have shown to you." (24)Abraham said, "I swear it." (25)Then Abraham complained to Abimelek about a well of water that Abimelek's servants had seized. (26)But Abimelek said, "I don't know who has done this. You did not tell me, and I heard about it only today." (27)So Abraham brought sheep and cattle and gave them to Abimelek, and the two men made a treaty. (28)Abraham set apart seven ewe lambs from the flock, (29)and Abimelek asked Abraham, "What is the meaning of these seven ewe lambs you have set apart by themselves?" (30)He replied, "Accept these seven lambs from my hand as a witness that I dug this well." (31)So that place was called Beersheba, because the two men swore an oath there. (32)After the treaty had been made at Beersheba, Abimelek and Phicol the commander of his forces returned to the land of the Philistines. (33)Abraham planted a tamarisk tree in Beersheba, and there he called on the name of the Lord, the Eternal God. (34)And Abraham stayed in the land of the Philistines for a long time.

Discussion Questions

Presented here are some questions for discussion with your Christian study group, women's group, or perhaps with the family over dinner. I don't feel qualified to present questions directed to a Jewish or Muslim audience, but feel free to explore these questions in the relevant terms of your own faith.

As Christians, feel free to explore and question in your discussions, but remember that at the end of the day, it is the Word of God in the Holy Bible that is our ultimate authority.

Question #1

Hagar would have most likely been a teenager at the time of her gifting to Sarai. Pharaoh's word would have been an absolute and unquestionable command. Given the highborn position of Hagar, if indeed she was the daughter of Pharaoh, discuss the emotional impact this decision would have on you if you were in her place, and how you would use your faith to persevere.

Question #2

One of the themes we explore in this story is the sense of lack of control. In our own lives we encounter situations both small and large that has control of actions and circumstances taken out of our hands. How do we respond to being at the whim of others in various situations (interpersonal, in social groups, in the workplace, confronting the law, etc.)? How can we use the lessons in the story of Hagar and other scripture to help us deal emotionally and spiritually with such situations?

Question #3

To discuss this question, please first read Isaiah 55:6-11.

In 1st Corinthians 2:11 we read *"For who knows a person's thoughts except their own spirit within them? In the same way no one knows the thoughts of God except the Spirit of God"*. It is not for us to know God's ways; it is for us to *trust* in God. Not knowing what is going to happen in certain situations can be scarier than actually knowing what is going to happen. Hagar was in this position many times. We find her in this situation first when she fled the house of Abraham while pregnant and then again after being banished with her son. Before the appearance of the angel of the Lord, she would have been in quite a state, as can be surmised from the narrative.

In our own life, we face crisis situations where our whole view and outlook of the future may hinge on a single event. This could be a job interview, facing termination from our job, a relationship struggle, a school application, a legal challenge, etc. Sometimes we face situations that make absolutely no sense to us until days, weeks, months, or sometimes years down the road. Then we can look back and see the divine hand of God moving things along according to his plan which, in the end (and sometimes that end is a long ways away) was to our benefit. Perhaps we find we were being used to benefit someone else in a very Godly way.

With these things in mind, when you are faced with the quandary of life going ways you simply can't fathom, but have not much choice other than to be swept along by the currents, how will you use your faith to be okay with this? How will you reconcile yourself to, "Thy will be done" and keep your faith strong and forefront? What scripture can you find in the Old Testament or New Testament that will help you with this? Perhaps you could make a promise to commit that scripture to memory so that it will always be available to you.

Question #4

In the story of Hagar, after she is banished and she finds herself with a dying son in the desert, the angel of the Lord speaks to her from heaven and saves her and her child. Truly this is a demonstration of God's love and presence in her life. This part of the story reminds me of the poem "Footprints in the Sand" by Mary Stevenson (1936). There have certainly been events in your life when at some point you realised that you had made it as far or as unscathed as you did simply because God was there and was intervening on your behalf. Share one of these stories with your group and give thanks together for His eternal presence, love, and attention to you.

Question #5

As we grow in our relationship with God and our experience with him in our life, either directly or through the Holy Spirit, we come to recognise times when His hand is at work. During the first season of the TV show the West Wing (S1E14, "Take this Sabbath Day"), actor Karl Malden appeared in his final role on television/film portraying a priest. In this episode, he related the following story:

A man living in a small town heard a warning on the radio that the river was overflowing and flood waters were going to rise and inundate the town. All residents were being encouraged to leave. The man chose not to leave and said, "I believe in God and trust in God, and God will save me". The waters did indeed start to rise and came to cover half his front steps. A man in a boat came by and beckoned the man to join him, leave his home, and be taken to safety. The man declined and said, "I believe in God and trust in God, and God will save me." A little while later the flood waters had risen quite a bit higher. They had entered his house and were halfway up to the ceiling. The man had retreated to the roof of the house to escape the flood waters. A helicopter came and hovered overhead. Using a bullhorn, the man in the helicopter beckoned to the man to climb the ladder so he could be taken to safety. The man declined and said, "I believe in God and trust in God, and God will save me." Shortly the flood waters rose over the house, the man was washed away and drowned. A bit angry and feeling let down, the man stood before the pearly gates and demanded an audience with God. God agreed to see the man and the man said to God, "I believed in you, I trusted in you, I waited for you to save me but you didn't". Then God said, "What are you doing here my son? I send you a warning, I sent you a boat, I sent you a helicopter. What were you waiting for?

How do you recognise God's movement in your life? To place our trust absolutely in God is a good thing. "Thy will be done" has deep and broad meaning to a Christian's life. However, that does not mean we are to sit back and let God deliver everything to us like a vending machine. We still have to do and build and act for ourselves with his guidance, support, and grace. So, in your life, discuss a time when you have recognised divine opportunities that were given to you. Did you recognise them as such at the time or only after the fact? How do you, now in your life, recognise when God has presented something to you or rather, what is it that makes you sit up and take notice of an opportunity or option that you think has been prepared for you by His hand?

Question #6

It has been stated by one source in this text that Abraham's travel to Egypt was a demonstration of a lack of faith. I have submitted for your consideration that in fact, Abraham's move to Egypt was divinely inspired, if not directly ordered, so that the events we have read about could take place.

Do you think that God may lead people into positions where they need His help so that He can demonstrate His love and His presence, or so that He can test your faith? Can you find other examples in the Bible that might reflect this?

Question #7

Consider the *Akeda*, the binding of the adolescent Isaac for sacrifice on the altar at the hand of his father, Abraham. What would have been the emotional and psychological impact on Isaac, realising his father was binding him to sacrifice him to God? In your life today, while an altar and blood sacrifice is definitely off the table (pardon the pun), what ways must you sacrifice or be willing to sacrifice your family for your devotion to God? How does this affect you? How does this affect your family? How do you reconcile with your family the fact that God comes first? Does God come first for you?

Question #8

Did the story of Hagar touch you in a profound or personal way? What elements of the story had the most meaning to you? What had the most impact on you? In what ways will you approach your life and your faith differently because of this story?

Question #9

David Guzik, pastor of Calvary Chapel in Santa Barbara, California made the following observation[51]:

"Abram, like most of us, found it easier to trust God in the far-off promises than in the right-now needs."

Why do you believe it is easier to believe in the far-off promises than the right-now needs? What do you think it would take for you to believe as strongly in the right-now needs? What is it that holds you back from this level of commitment and this level of expression of faith? What do you need to do to change this in yourself, in your family?

Jim Melanson

Poet, programmer, procrastinator, sci-fi geek, coffee snob, actor, and writer.

A devoted Christian, Jim is a quiet and thoughtful man who tends to think deeply and act slowly. Much of this inner reflection and self-assessment shows up in his writing. "Capturing what truly motivates us," is how Jim describes his approach to both fiction and non-fiction. This author has a direct, and sometimes *in-your-face* manner of writing. He tries to always use conversational language and make complex ideas understandable.

Jim read his first novel, by Laura Ingalls Wilder, at the age of eight; this began his love affair with the written word. Jim's first foray into personal writing, as a child, was poetry. These and other poetic scribblings provided the content for his first book, *I Apologize for Nothing*, published in April 2014.

Life, a child, a career with the Police Service, and a part-time business authoring software all got in the way of pursuing his desire to write. In 2013, Jim decided to pursue his creative yearnings, and he began writing for pleasure. Drawing on a solid work ethic from his experience authoring technical manuals and writing business proposals, Jim found writing for himself to be liberating and enjoyable. While working on his first fiction novel, he kept getting sidetracked by other ideas. He dusted off an old stage play he had written and published it under the title, *Mama's Slippers*, with the hopes of attracting production interest. In addition to non-fiction works on Christian topics, Jim also works on science fiction projects, including short stories and flash stories.

Originally hailing from the East Coast, Jim now lives just outside Cobourg, ON, with his two cats, Martin & Lewis.

End Notes

[1] Mindel, N. (n.d.). Abraham, Our Father. Retrieved from http://www.chabad.org/library/article_cdo/aid/112356/jewish/Abraham-Our-Father.htm

[2] Fischer, Michael M. J.; Mehdi Abedi (1990). *Debating Muslims: Cultural Dialogues in Postmodernity and Tradition.* Univ of Wisconsin Press. pp. 163–166. ISBN 978-0-299-12434-2.

[3] Whiston, W. (Trans.). (2008). *The works of Josephus: complete and unabridged.* Peabody, MA: Hendrickson .

[4] Kadari, T. (n.d.). Keturah: Midrash and Aggadah. Retrieved from https://jwa.org/encyclopedia/article/keturah-midrash-and-aggadah

[5] Shaviv, Y., Rabbi. (2003, November 22). Parashat Hayye Sarah 5764/ November 22, 2003. Retrieved from http://www.biu.ac.il/JH/Parasha/eng/chaye/sha.html

[6] Yonge, C. D. (Trans.). (1993). *The Works of Philo: Complete and Unabridged.* Hendrickson. pp. 305-306

[7] Whiston, W. (Trans.). (1987). *The Works of Josephus: Complete and Unabridged.* Peabody, MA: Hendrickson. p.44

[8] Biblehub.Com (n.d.) 2 Chronicles 12 Clarke's Commentary. Retrieved from http://biblehub.com/commentaries/clarke/2_chronicles/12.htm

[9] *Happy Arabia.* (n.d.). Retrieved from http://www.infoplease.com/dictionary/brewers/happy-arabia.html, Citing: *Dictionary of Phrase and Fable*, E. Cobham Brewer, 1894

[10] Guzik, D. (n.d.). Bible Commentaries: GENESIS 12 - GOD'S CALL OF ABRAM ABRAM IN EGYPT. Retrieved from https://www.studylight.org/commentaries/guz/genesis-12.html?print=yes; Used with permission.

[11] Universtiy of Pennsylvania (n.d.) *List of deities.* Retrieved from http://oracc.museum.upenn.edu/amgg/listofdeities/index.html

[12] Mosbergen, D. (2012, April 20). Renee Napier, Mother Of Drunk-Driving Accident Victim Meagan Napier, Forgives DUI Killer Eric Smallridge. *Huffington Post.* Retrieved from http://www.huffingtonpost.com/2012/04/20/renee-napier_n_1440809.html

[13] Daily Mail (2012, April 19) 'He's like a son to me': The unlikely friendship between a mother and the drunk driver who killed her daughter. *Daily Mail* Retrieved from http://www.dailymail.co.uk/news/article-2132152/Meagan-Napier-death-The-unlikely-friendship-mother-drunk-driver-killed-daughter.html

[14] Hartman, S. (2012, November 30). Mother's forgiveness gives convict second chance. Retrieved from http://www.cbsnews.com/news/mothers-forgiveness-gives-convict-second-chance/

[15] Wolf, J. (2015, November 29). Thriving Single Parents: the Stories Behind the Statistics. Retrieved https://www.thespruce.com/single-parenting-stories-and-statistics-2998072

[16] Gingerbread.Org.Uk (n.d.) Jonathan's story. Retrieved from https://gingerbread.org.uk/content/599/My-story---Single-dad-in-a-small-village

[17] Ussher, J., (1650). *The annals of the world deduced from the origin of time*. London: Printed by E. Tyler.

[18] Sperry, S. B. (1972, May). Hebrew Manners and Customs. Retrieved from https://www.lds.org/ensign/1972/05/hebrew-manners-and-customs?lang=eng

[19] Drey, P. R. (2002). *The Role of Hagar in Genesis 16*. Andrews University Seminary Studies, 40, No. 2, 184.

[20] Yehuda, E. B. (n.d.) *Ben Yehuda Dictionary and Thesaurus of the Hebrew Language: Complete International Centennial Edition 8 Volumes* (New York: Thomas Yoseloff, 1960), 3:7380.

[21] Lamm, M. (n.d.). The Jewish Marriage Ceremony - "According to the Laws of Moses and Israel". Retrieved from http://www.chabad.org/library/article_cdo/aid/465162/jewish/The-Jewish-Marriage-Ceremony.htm

[22] Answering-Islam.Org (n.d.) Hagar's legal status in Abraham's household. Retrieved from http://www.answering-islam.org/BibleCom/gen16-3.html

[23] Zaqantov, Y. (n.d.). What is the relationship between a Husband and a Wife? Retrieved from http://www.karaitejudaism.org/talks/Ish_and_ishah_relationship.htm

[24] Crawford, C. (n.d.). Mesopotamian Law. Retrieved February 16, 2017, from http://www.erasmatazz.com/library/the-

mind/history-of-thinking/early-civilization/mesopotamian-law.html

[25] King, L. W. (Trans) (n.d.) *The Avalon Project: Code of Hammurabi* Retrieved from
http://avalon.law.yale.edu/ancient/hamframe.asp

[26] Worldbank.Ord (n.d.) *Population, female (% of total).* Retrieved from
http://data.worldbank.org/indicator/SP.POP.TOTL.FE.ZS

[27] Stewart, D. (n.d.). Why Didn't God Condemn Lamech's Polygamy? Retrieved from
https://www.blueletterbible.org/faq/don_stewart/don_stewart_718.cfm

[28] Pope, C., Msgr. (2013, October 9). Polygamy in the Bible. Retrieved from
https://www.osv.com/MyFaith/Bible/Article/TabId/671/ArtMID/13714/ArticleID/13156/Polygamy-in-the-Bible.aspx

[29] Patterson, R. (2011, May 24). What About Polygamy in the Bible? Retrieved from
https://answersingenesis.org/family/marriage/what-about-polygamy-in-the-bible/

[30] Drey, P. R. (2002). *The Role of Hagar in Genesis 16.* Andrews University Seminary Studies, 40, No. 2, 184.

[31] Yehuda, E. B. (n.d.) *Ben Yehuda Dictionary and Thesaurus of the Hebrew Language: Complete International Centennial Edition 8 Volumes Edition* (New York: Thomas Yoseloff, 1960), 3:7380.

[32] Jewish Encyclopedia *(n.d.) Hagar*. Retrieved from http://www.jewishencyclopedia.com/articles/7021-hagar

[33] Smith, W (1970). Smith's Bible Dictionary, entry for Shur. AJ Holman & Co.

[34] Dr. J. Vernon McGee. (2005). Genesis 16: 11-16. Thru the Bible Radio. Retrieved from
https://www.blueletterbible.org/audio_video/mcgee_j_vernon/Gen/Genesis.cfm#Genesis_16_11_16

[35] *First Mention Principle Definition.* (n.d.). Retrieved from http://www.biblestudy.org/beginner/definition-of-christian-terms/first-mention-principle.html

[36] Jon Courson. (2006). Genesis 16-17. Searchlight Ministries. (1998)
http://www.joncourson.com/teaching/teachingsplay.asp?book=g

enesis&teaching=W3014&mediatype=audiofile

[37] Gill, J. (1748-1763). John Gill's Exposition of the Entire Bible: Genesis Chapter 16. Retrieved from http://www.sacred-texts.com/bib/cmt/gill/gen016.htm

[38] Scripture4All Publishing. (2015, July 28). ISA Basic (Version 3.0.2) [Computer software]. Retrieved http://www.scripture4all.org/

[39] Sinnott, A. (2010). *Breastfeeding older children*. London: Free Association Books.

[40] Gill, J. (1748-1763). John Gill's Exposition of the Entire Bible: Genesis Chapter 22. Retrieved from http://www.sacred-texts.com/bib/cmt/gill/gen022.htm

[41] Pastor Dave Elkins (2012). Personal correspondence. Calvary Chapel. Dayton, OH

[42] Fletcher, E. (2006). Beersheba, ancient Bible city. Retrieved from http://www.womeninthebible.net/bible-archaeology/city-of-beersheba/

[43] Jewish Virtual Library (n.d.) *The Negev Desert.* Retrieved from http://www.jewishvirtuallibrary.org/the-negev-desert

[44] Lutz, E. (2011, March 07). What Is the Water of Life? Retrieved from https://answersingenesis.org/answers/biblical-authority-devotional/what-is-the-water-of-life/

[45] Tverberg, L. (2015, October 06). What is Living Water? Retrieved from http://ourrabbijesus.com/articles/living-water/

[46] Stanley, C. (n.d.). What "Living Water" Did Jesus Offer? Retrieved from http://www.jesus.org/life-of-jesus/teaching-and-messages/what-living-water-did-jesus-offer.html

[47] Bereishit Rabbah 61:4 Reprinted in, e.g., *The Midrash: Midrash Rabbah with an Annotated, Interpretive Elucidation and Additional Insights*. Edited by Chaim Malinowitz, volume 2, page 31.

[48] Wojo, R. (2013, October 01). 14 Bible Verses For When I Can't Understand God's Plan. Retrieved from http://rachelwojo.com/bible-verses-when-i-cant-understand-gods-plan/

[49] Walvoord, J. F. (1969). *Jesus Christ our Lord*. Chicago, IL: Moody Publishers.

[50] Coffman, J. B. (n.d.) *Overview - James Burton Coffman Commentaries on the Bible*. Retrieved from https://www.studylight.org/commentaries/bcc.html

[51] Guzik, D (2006) Guzik Bible Commentary: Genesis 12. BibleHub.Com. Retrieved from http://biblehub.com/commentaries/guzik/genesis/12.htm